From Pearl Harbor to Okinawa

FROM PEARL HARBOR TO OKINAWA

The War in the Pacific: 1941–1945

BY BRUCE BLIVEN, JR.

MAPS BY FRITZ AND STEPHEN KREDEL

RANDOM HOUSE • NEW YORK

Photograph credits: Department of Defense (Marine Corps), endpapers, pages ii-iii, vi, 75 bottom, 95 top, 100, 119, 129 bottom, 155, 160 bottom, 175; U. S. Air Force, 134, 164, 182; U. S. Army, 50, 107, 138, 151, 160 top, 187, 188; U. S. Coast Guard, 129 top; U. S. Navy, 2, 7, 17, 43, 59, 95 bottom, 170; Wide World Photos, 22, 27, 70, 75 top, 113.

This title was originally catalogued by the Library of Congress as follows:

Bliven, Bruce, 1916–
　　From Pearl Harbor to Okinawa; the war in the Pacific, 1941–1945. Maps by Fritz and Stephen Kredel. New York, Random House [1960]

　　　192 p.　illus.　22 cm.　(Landmark books [94])

　　1. World War, 1939–1945—Pacific Ocean.　I. Title.

D767.B55　　　　　　　　940.5426　　　　　60—10019 ‡

　　Library of Congress　　　　　[a68r61q⅜]

Trade Ed.: ISBN: 0- 394-80394-9　　　Lib. Ed.: ISBN: 0-394-90394-3

Manufactured in the United States of America

for Naomi,
with love and thanks

Contents

From Pearl Harbor to Okinawa

1

The Japanese Attack

At 6:30 on the morning of Sunday, December 7, 1941, the crew of the United States Navy auxiliary ship, the *Antares,* saw something almost unbelievable. The *Antares* was towing an ammunition barge not far outside the entrance to Pearl Harbor, which is on the south side of Oahu Island, Hawaii. Pearl Harbor was the United States Pacific Fleet's main base. What the men on watch saw was a periscope and part of a small, oval conning tower. As far as they could make out, the *Antares* was being followed by an unidentifiable, submerged submarine.

This was astonishing because the *Antares* was plowing along through a restricted area. Submarines were not allowed to go there unless they had special permission, and then all patrol ships and planes guarding the base were notified to expect them. To make matters more mysterious, the periscope didn't look like one of ours. There were no visible identifying letters or numbers. Under these circumstances, the stranger had to be treated like an enemy vessel. But the United States wasn't at war. Officially, we had no enemies.

The *Antares* notified the nearby patrol destroyer *Ward*. This wasn't the first submarine report the *Ward* had received that day. At 4:05 A.M. the minesweeper *Condor* had reported sighting a moving periscope in the same area. But the *Ward*, misled by the wording of the *Condor's* radio message, had hunted for a submarine in the wrong place—and naturally hadn't found it.

Now the *Ward* saw what the *Antares* had seen, and was steaming over at full speed for a closer look. So had a Navy patrol plane, an amphibious Catalina, which dropped markers. As soon as the captain of the *Ward* had studied the odd conning tower through his binoculars, he did what his standing orders required: he attacked.

"Commence firing!" he ordered. The time was 6:45 A.M. The *Ward's* first shell was high, and it plunged into the sea far beyond the submarine. The second shot was a direct hit on the conning tower. Immediately afterward, the *Ward* swept past her target, almost running the submarine down. As she left it behind, the *Ward* dropped four depth charges off her stern. The *Ward's* chief torpedoman said later that the crippled sub "seemed to wade right into the first one." A towering geyser of gray-green water shot into the air. The mysterious submarine was finished.

The first shots in the war in the Pacific between Japan and the United States—a war that hadn't yet been declared—had been fired.

The *Ward* had done what she was supposed to do in such an emergency, but for the next hour the ship's officers were afraid that they might have sunk an American ship.

The idea that the strange submarine was leading the way for a tremendous Japanese strike against Pearl Harbor—an air raid, primarily—calculated to wreck the United States Pacific Fleet with one devastating blow never crossed their minds. Yet by seven o'clock the first wave of Vice Admiral Chuichi Nagumo's torpedo bombers, dive bombers, and fighter planes, which had been launched from six aircraft carriers at a point in the ocean 200 miles north of Oahu Island, were already streaking south. Pearl Harbor was their target.

Nagumo's powerful task force also included two battleships and an assortment of cruisers, destroyers, submarines, and tankers. Starting on November 26th, it had sailed a northerly course to Hawaii from Hitokippu Bay in the Japanese Islands. None of our scouting planes and ships had seen it.

The submarine the *Ward* had sunk belonged to a second Japanese force assisting Nagumo's main effort. It was a midget that had been launched from a big Japanese submarine, one of twenty-eight that had quietly moved in from the southwest and taken up stations in the waters around Oahu Island. There were four other midgets like it. (Most of the other big submarines carried scouting planes which they could catapult off their decks.) Each of the midget subs, manned by two sailors, carried two torpedoes. The idea was that they might be able to slip through the antisubmarine nets at the entrance to Pearl Harbor, and sink a warship or two, although that was almost certainly a suicidal mission. One of the midgets did sneak into the harbor a little later in the day; but before it could do any serious damage, it was rammed, run down, and depth-bombed by the United States destroyer *Monaghan*. The others, including the *Ward's* victim, ran aground or were sunk without accomplishing anything. The big Japanese submarines were waiting to see whether any of our fleet would

Crewmen of a Japanese aircraft carrier wave as planes depart for the surprise attack on Pearl Harbor.

A Japanese midget submarine stranded off Oahu Island.

survive the air attack and escape from the harbor into the open sea. If so, the subs intended to torpedo them as they made their getaway.

All that was yet to come. For the moment, there was the *Ward's* puzzling encounter to consider. Higher headquarters, when it got the action report, wasted precious time trying to figure out what it could mean, and in deciding what to do about it.

Minutes later—at 7:02 A.M.—a mobile radar unit operated by the Army, which was set up near Kahuku Point at the northern tip of Oahu Island, picked up the approaching Japanese planes. They were still 130 miles away. The two privates operating the radar —one of them was teaching the other how to work it —were greatly impressed; the blip on the screen was the biggest they had ever seen. They tracked the planes for thirty-seven minutes, until the flight was only twenty-two miles away. Then they lost them in a "dead zone" caused by the surrounding hills. All this time they tried to stir up some interest at the Army's General Information Center, but the duty officer there kept calm. He felt sure that the planes were our own B-17 bombers flying in from California.

If the sinking of the midget submarine and the radar sighting had been interpreted properly, the fifty minutes' advance warning they provided would have allowed our fighter planes to take to the air, and some of the oncoming Japanese bombers could surely have been intercepted.

If an alert had been sounded at seven o'clock, all the ships in the harbor could have called their crews to battle stations. Some of them could have been under way, thus making themselves difficult targets. Our battleships' anti-aircraft gun crews could have been set to shoot as the Japanese bombers came in, skimming low over the water, to make their torpedo-bomb runs.

But that wasn't the way it happened. There was no general alarm until the Japanese bombs began to fall. Most of the fighting men at Pearl Harbor were just waking up or getting up, in a leisurely manner, to what they thought would be the ordinary routine of an ordinary Sunday morning.

Inside Pearl Harbor lay the great obstacle to Japan's dreams of conquest: the United States Pacific Fleet. A few ships were elsewhere, but eight of the nine great battleships were on hand. They were the backbone of the Fleet's strength. The harbor contained some seventy warships. Besides the battleships there were two heavy cruisers, six light cruisers, twenty-nine destroyers, five submarines, a gunboat, nine mine layers, and ten mine sweepers. Then there were about two dozen auxiliary ships like tenders, oilers, tugs, ammunition and supply ships. The entire fleet lay peacefully at anchor—with some few important exceptions.

Army, Navy, and Marine planes were stationed on various airstrips all over the island. There were more than 200 Army planes, although a number of them were out of commission awaiting repairs. The Marines had fifty planes, mostly scout-bombers, and about 150 Navy planes were on hand. Again, with a few exceptions, almost all of them were on the ground.

A few seconds before 7:55, the first Japanese plane, diving out of the sky, roared over Ford Island, which sits in the middle of the harbor, and dropped its bomb on a seaplane ramp.

Rear Admiral W. R. Furlong was the S.O.P.A. (the senior officer present afloat). The moment he saw the Japanese Rising Sun insignia painted on the side of the bomber—the "meatball," in Navy slang—he ordered all ships to sortie. That meant that they were to start moving and leave the harbor immediately. Unhappily, with the exception of one destroyer, the *Helm,* none of them could obey the command, because it takes time to get up steam and get under way.

A minute or two later, the signal tower at Pearl Harbor telephoned Admiral Husband E. Kimmel's headquarters. (Admiral Kimmel was the commander in chief of the Pacific Fleet.)

DETROIT

RALEIGH

UTAH

TANGIER

FORD ISLAND

NEVADA
ARIZONA
VESTAL
TENNESSEE
W-VIRGINIA
MARYLAND
OKLAHOMA
NEOSHO
CALIFORNIA

NEW ORLEANS
SAN FRANCISCO
HONOLULU

PENNSYLVANIA

TANK FARM

TANK FARM

HICKAM FIELD

ANTI TORPEDO
AND BOAT NET   XXXXXXXXXXXXXXXX

PEARL HARBOR
AT 7:55
7 DECEMBER 1941

MAMALA   BAY

"Enemy air raid," the tower said. And then it added, "Not drill."

On every ship, the raucous sounds of klaxons called their crews to battle stations. At the same time, with one deadly boom after another, the Japanese bombs continued to fall.

The Japanese aviators knew exactly what they were doing. Their attack plan, though intricate, was timed to a split second. The seven American battleships, moored in a tidy row to concrete pillars off the south shore of Ford Island, were their number-one target. (The eighth battleship, the *Pennsylvania,* was in dry dock just across the way.)

There were forty torpedo bombers, fifty dive bombers, fifty high-level bombers and fifty fighters in the first wave of planes from the Japanese carriers, and they swarmed in from every side. The torpedo bombers skimmed low, launching their missiles from just fifty feet off the calm surface of the water. Once these torpedoes hit the water, they drove along under their own power and struck our ships below the water-line—a most devastating blow. High-level and dive bombers were right behind the torpedo bombers, hitting our ships' topsides and raking their decks with machine-gun fire. The Japanese fighter planes concentrated on our airfields, blazing away at our parked planes on the ground, firing on crewmen and pilots unlucky enough to get within the machine-gunners' sights.

No sooner had the Japanese fliers dropped their deadly loads than they turned, at the end of their bombing runs, and came back to strafe the battle-ships' decks, killing our sailors as they scrambled to man anti-aircraft posts and to fight the fires which were breaking out almost everywhere.

Half an hour after the first bomb was dropped, all seven American battleships were seriously damaged. The *Arizona* was a flaming torch. The *Oklahoma*, hit by three torpedoes in rapid-fire succession, and then another pair as she rolled over on her side, was al-most upside down—and 415 of her officers and men were killed or missing. The *West Virginia* was sunk. The *California* was going down. Two deep-running torpedoes had hit her just fore and aft of her bridge; salt water had gotten into her fuel system; she had lost light and power; and, to make matters worse, a bomb then exploded below her deck, setting off the anti-aircraft ammunition magazine.

The Japanese had succeeded in their main mis-sion: the Pacific Fleet's Battle Force was all but wrecked.

The United States air forces had taken an equally bad beating. Most of the twenty-nine Navy patrol bombers on Ford Island had been demolished in a matter of minutes, and so had twenty-seven of the thirty-three PBY's at Kaneohe, the Navy field on Oahu's east coast. Forty-five of the forty-seven Marine planes at Ewa Field—Wildcat fighters, scout-bombers, and utility planes—had either been destroyed completely or put out of commission. Two-thirds of the Army's fighter planes on Wheeler Field had been reduced to junk. Most of them had been parked in tidy straight lines around the landing strips, with their wing tips almost touching.

The Japanese dive bombers had swept down those lines, flying at no more than hangar-top level. Their high-explosive bombs could tear a fighter plane apart like kindling wood, and their machine guns, loaded with incendiary bullets, ripped into any planes the bombs missed. Many of our fighters had tanks full of gasoline. These had caught fire, or exploded, spreading the damage even farther. Wheeler Field was blanketed with clouds of thick, oily smoke, making it extra hard to separate the burning planes from those that still might be able to fly. Despite everything, a few of our pilots—about fourteen of them—managed to take off, but not until the worst of the Japanese attack had ended. Hickam Field, where the Army's B-18 and B-17 bombers were parked, had been a wreck after the first five minutes, though by a miracle four of the big planes were almost unscratched.

From a flier's point of view, there is something horrible about having your plane destroyed on the ground. Our airmen went crazy with rage when they saw it happening. It was too late to do anything that would make any real difference, but many of them did what they could. Some tore the machine guns out of their wrecked planes, and tried to mount them on anything handy—workbenches and, in one case, even an ash can.

But, with a few exceptions, American air strength on Oahu was as helpless as the Fleet it was supposed to be protecting.

The initial Japanese attack had been so successful that the 9:00 A.M. follow-up air strike—designed to mop up whatever the first wave might have missed— had comparatively little to do.

There were 170 Japanese planes in the second attack, almost as many as in the first wave. American anti-aircraft fire had improved, and a handful of our fighters were in the air trying against overwhelming odds to fight back. But the Japanese added a few lethal blows to their fantastic score. Our battleship *Nevada,* the last or easternmost of the ships in the battleship row, had been luckier than most, and was being handled magnificently by a Reserve Lieutenant Commander, Francis J. Thomas, who happened to be the senior officer aboard.

The *Nevada* had been hit with one torpedo, which had torn a huge hole in her side, forty-five feet long and thirty feet high. She had also suffered two or three bomb hits. Nevertheless, at about half-past eight, Commander Thomas had decided to try to move his ship down the channel and out into the open sea. The Chief Boatswain, E. J. Hill, jumped onto the mooring, cast off the lines with Japanese machine-gun fire splattering all around him, and then swam back to his ship as she was starting to move.

A flight of second-wave Japanese dive bombers, heading for the *Pennsylvania* in dry dock, saw what the *Nevada* was trying to do, and concentrated on her instead. There was no chance of escaping them. The *Nevada* took half a dozen more hits, as the geysers of water from the near misses drenched her decks. She was flooding fast. If she sank in the channel, nothing would be able to get in or out of Pearl Harbor except the smallest ships. Two tugs hurried to her assistance, and the *Nevada*, billowing clouds of smoke from her several fires, was deliberately beached on the hard bottom at Waipio Point.

The follow-up Japanese attack also scored a direct hit on the battleship *Pennsylvania*. Since she was already in dry dock, that wasn't too bad. Repairs would be fairly simple. Much worse was the fact that the two destroyers ahead of the *Pennsylvania,* in the same

The severly damaged battleship USS Nevada (in background) a few minutes after leaving her berth.

Planes in flames after the attack on Pearl Harbor by Japanese dive bombers.

dock, were set on fire and the fires exploded their torpedoes. By the time the flames were brought under control, both destroyers were reduced to smoldering wrecks.

The whole bow of another destroyer, the *Shaw*, was blown off when fires reached her forward ammunition magazine, and the light cruiser *Honolulu* was damaged by a near miss.

By 9:45 A.M. the battle was over.

No war has ever started with such a victory for one side at the very beginning of the hostilities.

Eighteen American warships—including seven of the eight battleships—were sunk or badly damaged. The cruisers *Raleigh*, *Helena*, and *Honolulu* were crippled. Three destroyers were frightful wrecks.

Out of the total of about 400 American airplanes, 188 had been destroyed and another 159 damaged.

Our casualties were appalling. When the *Arizona* sank, after taking at least eight bomb hits in addition to the damage done to her by torpedoes, she settled so fast that more than a thousand sailors were trapped below decks where they were either drowned or burned to death. That was by far the worst single disaster. It accounted for almost half of the total number of 2,403 of Americans killed, missing, or mortally wounded during the day. Another 1,178 were wounded.

In fact, the Navy lost almost three times as many men in this one attack as it lost by enemy action in the Spanish-American War and the First World War combined.

All this had been accomplished at the trivial cost to the Japanese of twenty-nine planes, fifty-five airmen, and six submarines.

It was hard to find comfort in our terrible defeat, but actually the Japanese had neglected some vital targets. For instance, they had ignored Pearl Harbor's ship-repair facilities, with the result that our less badly damaged warships went back into action in a short time. They had overlooked the base power plant which supplied the electricity that ran all the repair machinery. They hadn't bombed the "farm" of fuel-oil storage tanks which were filled to capacity. An American admiral estimated that if the fuel had gone up in flames, the loss would have delayed our counter-attack longer than did the destruction of our battle-ships.

And then, the fact that our three carriers—the *Enterprise,* the *Saratoga,* and the *Lexington*—had been off on various missions, out of harm's way, was a great piece of good luck.

The next day, Monday, December 8th, the United States declared war on Japan. Most Americans, at first, had hardly been able to believe the news of the

Japanese attack. Many of them had been listening to the Sunday afternoon broadcast of the New York Philharmonic Orchestra when the first flash came. But as soon as this country's citizens understood that the report was not a hoax, an amazing wave of public agreement swept the nation.

When the Senate and the House of Representatives met in joint session at twenty-five minutes past noon, there was almost complete approval of what everybody knew Congress was about to do.

At 12:30 P.M. President Franklin D. Roosevelt, looking serious, began to ask for a declaration of war: "Yesterday, December 7, 1941—a date that will live in infamy—the United States of America was suddenly and deliberately attacked by naval and air forces of the Empire of Japan . . ."

"Infamy," which means dishonor or disgrace, was exactly the right word. As the President reminded his audience, Japan's sneak attack had come in the midst of diplomatic conversations with the United States— talks the Japanese had requested. Japan had tricked us into believing that she hoped for continued peace in the Pacific. She had been preparing the Pearl Harbor strike for months while, in Washington, her representatives insisted that Japan wanted to negotiate about the objections we had raised to what she was doing in the Far East.

Japan's armed forces were on the offensive throughout the entire Pacific, and President Roosevelt proceeded to check off a list of the places that had been attacked without warning:

". . . In addition, American ships have been reported torpedoed on the high seas between San Francisco and Honolulu.

"Yesterday the Japanese Government also launched an attack against Malaya.

"Last night Japanese forces attacked Hong Kong.

"Last night Japanese forces attacked Guam.

"Last night Japanese forces attacked the Philippine Islands.

"Last night the Japanese attacked Wake Island.

"This morning the Japanese attacked Midway Island.

". . . Hostilities exist. There is no blinking at the fact that our people, our territory, and our interests are in grave danger.

"With confidence in our armed forces—with the unbounded determination of our people—we will gain the inevitable triumph—so help us God.

"I ask that the Congress declare that since the un-

Declaring Japan guilty of an "unprovoked and dastardly" attack, President Roosevelt asks Congress for a declaration of war.

provoked and dastardly attack by Japan on Sunday, December 7th, a state of war has existed between the United States and the Japanese Empire."

The members of the Senate returned to their own chamber in the Capitol. Both houses, within minutes adopted the resolution the President had asked for. At 4:10 that same afternoon, the President signed the declaration. The United States was formally at war with Japan.

Three days later—a few hours before we were ready to declare war on them—Germany and Italy declared war on the United States.

We were belligerents in the greatest military struggle in recorded history, the Second World War, which was already two years and three months old. All together, seventy nations, and more than three-quarters of the earth's population, were involved. More than 100 million men and women belonged to the armed forces of both sides, and before the enemy was finally defeated, in 1945, the military casualties (killed and wounded) alone added up to about twenty million. There are no reliable figures for the tens of millions of additional civilian casualties. One expert has guessed that the Second World War cost $1,000,000,-000,000,000 (one quadrillion dollars), though the truth is that the real cost of war is too frightful to measure in terms of money.

If, possibly, this terrible waste might at some point in history have been avoided, by December, 1941, it was far too late for the world to do anything except resist the military might that Adolf Hitler of Germany, Benito Mussolini of Italy, and Hideki Tojo of Japan had set in motion.

We and our allies were determined to fight until the two European dictators and their Japanese partner were completely destroyed—an unlimited war on a global scale.

Most Americans, as their country entered the war, underestimated Japan's strength. The ordinary citizen had considerable respect for Hitler's war machine; Hitler's expert propagandists had worked hard to plant it in our minds. But most Americans imagined that Tojo had gone mad in the Pacific, and it was some time before the public appreciated the military significance of our defeat at Pearl Harbor. If Hitler and Mussolini could be beaten, most people thought, Japan would prove a comparatively easy adversary.

Our Joint Chiefs of Staff had no such optimistic illusion. Japan's war plan made good military sense, from a Japanese point of view.

Tojo and his colleagues were making just one fatal mistake. They had completely miscalculated American reaction to their treacherous attack, for they thought that defeat in Hawaii and the Philippines would persuade us to give up before we had really started to fight back.

The thought never crossed the average American's mind.

2

The Fall of the Philippines

Japan's bold offensive was a success everywhere from Hawaii to Malaya. The area in which she had attacked covers more than one-third of the globe. (The Pacific Ocean alone is so big that it could hold twenty countries the size of the United States.) And Japanese fighting forces were in action on December 7th from one end of the theater to the other. Tojo had thrown more than one thousand warships into these battles. Hundreds of his troop transports, loaded with hundreds of thousands of Japanese invasion troops, were headed for a dozen different points.

At Midway Island, 1300 miles west of Pearl Harbor, our marines were shelled by a pair of Japanese destroyers, and then bombed and strafed by Japanese planes.

At Wake Island, 1200 miles southwest of Midway, a squadron of Japanese bombers swept down on the airfield and the cluster of buildings around it. Our garrison force there was made up of 422 marines. Their situation—since they couldn't be reinforced—was hopeless. Incredibly, they managed to hold out for more than two weeks despite constant pounding from the air and from the sea. Wake fell to the Japanese invaders on December 23rd.

Guam, 1300 miles southwest of Wake, was the only island in the Marianas not under Japanese mandate. The United States Navy station there, as well as all our other military installations on the island, was smashed by a combination of air bombardment and pounding by Japanese naval gunfire. Our 424 navy men and marines, like our men on Wake, had no chance of stopping the Japanese invaders.

Hong Kong, Great Britain's seaport on the China coast, was overrun in just eighteen days. Four British and two Canadian army battalions fought as best they could, but they were pitifully short of air support. They had only six old-fashioned planes, which were damaged at the very beginning of the Japanese air raids. The Japanese 38th Division, with better training, better equipment, and far better support

Despite the arrival of Canadian reinforcements, Hong Kong fell in just eighteen days.

both in the air and on the sea, couldn't be stopped. The British lost 12,000 men, more than four times as many casualties as the victorious Japanese.

At Singapore, on the southern tip of Malaya, there was another British disaster. The British naval base there was so strongly fortified that for twenty years British citizens had believed it could withstand any attack. But the Malay Peninsula, a steaming jungle rich in tin deposits and full of rubber plantations, was a land the Japanese war lords felt they had to have. Singapore guarded the way to the Indian Ocean. In Japanese hands it would also be an important step toward the rich islands of Sumatra, Java, and Borneo.

Like Hong Kong, Singapore was perilously short of planes. At least 336 first-class aircraft were needed and only 158 were on hand. And the British mistakenly imagined that the dense jungle north of Singapore protected their stronghold. They felt so secure that the British troops, in addition to lacking air strength, tanks, and field artillery, hadn't had realistic training in the difficult art of jungle warfare.

The jungle was far less of a barrier than the British hoped. Starting on December 8th, the Japanese moved south with amazing speed. The four attacking divisions of the Japanese Twenty-fifth army had strong naval and air support, and the Japanese established air bases close to Malaya's northern boundary so that planes could bomb ahead of General Tomoyuki Yamashita's two infantry columns as they advanced down the Malay Peninsula. The Japanese were very skillful. Many of them were battle-wise veterans. They wore lightweight uniforms and carried little equipment; they could slip through the jungle like ghosts. British positions were infiltrated, surrounded, and overrun before the defenders knew what was happening. Many of the Japanese thrusts were made at night, when the British more or less expected the fighting to stop.

The British commander, General A. E. Percival, was soon forced to fall back, and by the end of January his troops had retreated from the peninsula to Singapore Island itself. They fought hard to prevent the Japanese from crossing the Strait of Johore—British casualties were close to 140,000 killed and wounded—but Singapore's anti-landing preparations, like everything else about its defenses, proved inadequate. Singapore surrendered on February 15, 1942.

At the beginning of the hopeless battle for Singapore, Great Britain lost two of her best ships. The *Prince of Wales,* one of the newest, most powerful warships in the world, and the battlecruiser *Repulse* had sailed out of Singapore on December 8th in the hope of interrupting the Japanese landing operations. Now they both were at the bottom of the South China

Sea, victims of the same deadly weapon that had caused such damage at Pearl Harbor—the Japanese torpedo bomber.

"In all the war, I never received a more direct shock," the British Prime Minister, Winston Churchill, wrote later. . . . "There were no British or American capital ships in the Indian Ocean or the Pacific except the American survivors of Pearl Harbor. . . . Over all this vast expanse of waters Japan was supreme, and we everywhere were weak and naked."

Japan was interested, above all, in seizing French Indochina, Thailand, Burma, Malaya, and the Netherlands Indies, especially Sumatra, Borneo, Java, and Celebes. They could give her the raw materials—especially oil—she needed in order to dominate the entire Far East.

The Japanese had been at war with China since 1937. Japan had seized Manchuria and had occupied a considerable part of Chinese territory, but China was proving a more difficult opponent than the Japanese had expected. The Chinese Central Government, headed by Generalissimo Chiang Kai-shek, had won almost no battles, but it had been able to trade space for time, retreating farther and farther to the west, and avoiding a really decisive engagement. The Chinese capital had moved 500 miles, from Hankow to Chungking.

Japan was the aggressor, and for ten years the world had disapproved of what she was doing.

The United States was providing Chiang with military supplies, but for the most part China had been left alone with her problem of self-defense.

On the other hand, Japan's conquests were costing far more than she could afford. When Hitler attacked the Low Countries, sweeping through Holland, Belgium, and France, and handing the British army a terrible defeat along the way, Japan saw her opportunity. It was the perfect time, Japan thought, to steal French, English, and Dutch possessions in the Far East. The United States was the only great power that could stand in her way.

That was the logic that had been behind Premier Tojo's daring assault on the United States Pacific Fleet at Pearl Harbor. Hitler's invasion army was only forty miles outside Moscow. Western Europe lay in defeat. Except for the fact that the German air force had been unable to beat the Royal Air Force, the British Isles seemed terribly vulnerable. None of our allies could offer us much help in the Pacific.

Tojo thought that once our Pacific Fleet was destroyed, and Japan had conquered all the South Pacific, including the Philippines, Japan would be able to establish a line of military strongpoints around everything north of Australia. This "fence" would stretch between Burma on the west and Wake Island on the east. Such a "defensive perimeter," Tojo imagined, would protect his ill-gotten gains. By the time the Allies could do anything about striking back, Tojo hoped, they would be too discouraged to try.

According to the Japanese timetable for conquest, capture of the Philippines was supposed to be easier than that of Malaya and Singapore. The Philippine defenses were certainly not everything one might have wished. The United States had promised the Philippine Commonwealth complete independence by 1946. Lieutenant General Douglas MacArthur was working on a plan to make the islands so tough that no aggressor would want to pay the price of attacking them. But these preparations were far from complete.

When the Japanese struck, shortly after noon on December 8th, the Philippine army needed at least twice as many trained soldiers as it had. It was also short of equipment of all kinds. But there were a few American units on hand. The largest was a regular army outfit, the Philippine Division, commanded by Major General Jonathan M. Wainwright. There were some up-to-date airplanes, including thirty-five B-17 bombers and about one hundred P-40 fighter planes. And the small United States Asiatic Fleet, commanded by Admiral Thomas Hart, was composed of three cruisers, twenty-nine submarines, thirteen old-fashioned destroyers left over from the First World War, and six motor torpedo boats.

General MacArthur, with his headquarters in Manila, commanded all the Army forces in the Far East. He had been called back to duty in July, 1941, after completing a distinguished thirty-eight-year military career. He was sixty-one years old. He had been first in his class at West Point (1903), President Theodore Roosevelt's military aide, a hero of the 42nd Infantry Division during the First World War, the Superintendent of the Military Academy (1919-22), and, from 1930 to 1935, the Army Chief of Staff.

On top of all that, MacArthur had spent a remarkable amount of time in the Far East, starting with his very first assignment after graduation from West Point. He had served in the Philippines, and he had even acted as an aide to his father, General Arthur MacArthur, who was the United States military observer with the Japanese army during the war between Japan and Russia in 1905.

After his retirement, MacArthur had gone to work for the Philippine Commonwealth, and had been made field marshal of the Philippine army.

It is safe to say that no one in our armed forces was better acquainted with the ground he was defending or the army attacking it. Even before the war in the Pacific began, MacArthur's military record had entitled him to a place among the distinguished men in American military history. The number of military errors MacArthur had made could have been counted on the fingers of one hand—and very likely with fingers to spare. But when the surprise Japanese air attack hit the Philippines at noon on December 8th, it exposed a shocking blunder. Our bombers and fighters were sitting on the ground, as helpless as our air forces on Oahu Island had been.

The terrible part was that MacArthur's headquarters had been warned ten hours in advance of the Japanese attack. The Philippines had heard about Pearl Harbor as soon as it happened. Some planes had actually taken to the air for safety's sake and had then landed again. But the whole Philippine air force was off guard when the Japanese bombers and fighter planes arrived. After the smoke had cleared away, half of MacArthur's air power—his main defense against Japanese invasion—had been destroyed.

Powerful Japanese assault forces were steaming from Formosa toward their Philippine objectives. Manila, and the military establishments there, were the final Japanese goal. But General Masaharu Homma, the Japanese commander, did not intend to land with his main strength at Lingayen Gulf, which is a little more than 100 miles north of Manila, until he could provide air support for his infantrymen. He planned half a dozen preliminary landings, mostly on the coast of northern Luzon Island, in order to capture airstrips.

MacArthur had to save his strength for the main Japanese attack, and Homma's first landings, some of them entirely unopposed, went smoothly. We had one small success which gave the hearts of all Americans a lift they badly needed. But when the records were all in, it turned out to have been much less important than we thought at the time.

While the Japanese were coming ashore on December 10th, two of MacArthur's bombers which had managed to survive repeated air attacks on Clark Field took off to do what they could to raise havoc among the Japanese troop transports off Aparri, on Luzon's northern tip. The second of these planes was commanded by a 26-year-old West Pointer, Captain Colin P. Kelly, Jr., and his bombardier was Corporal Meyer Levin of Brooklyn, New York. Both bombers scored hits. The first plane dropped one of its 600-pound bombs on a Japanese transport. Kelly and his crew, paying no attention to heavy anti-aircraft fire, attacked what they thought was the 29,000-ton Japanese battleship *Haruna*. (The *Haruna* was actually hundreds of miles away, supporting the enemy drive toward Singapore.)

As Kelly flew away, the Japanese ship—whichever one

it really was—looked as if she would sink, but we know now that she did not.

Just before Kelly's plane got back to Clark Field, two Japanese fighters jumped it. Cannon and machine-gun bullets riddled the fuselage, killing the flight engineer. The oxygen system was set on fire. Kelly ordered all the surviving members of his crew to bail out, which they did. But before Kelly himself could jump, the B-17 exploded. Kelly's body was later recovered from the plane's wreckage on the ground.

Whether our two planes had done the Japanese any serious damage or not, the whole country was thrilled by news of our aviators' bravery.

In just a few days' time Homma controlled Luzon's northern coast—airfields included—as far south as San Fernando. Manila, blacked out by night, and in an understandable state of civilian panic, waited for the Japanese to make their next move. MacArthur seemed calm and almost optimistic, even though the remnants of his bomber force, having no safe place to land, had withdrawn to Australia, leaving only a handful of fighters in the Philippines. And, once the Japanese controlled the air over the Philippines, Admiral Hart ordered most of his fleet to retire, feeling that they should be saved to fight another day. His submarines, which were less vulnerable to air attack than surface vessels, stayed behind. So did two of the an-

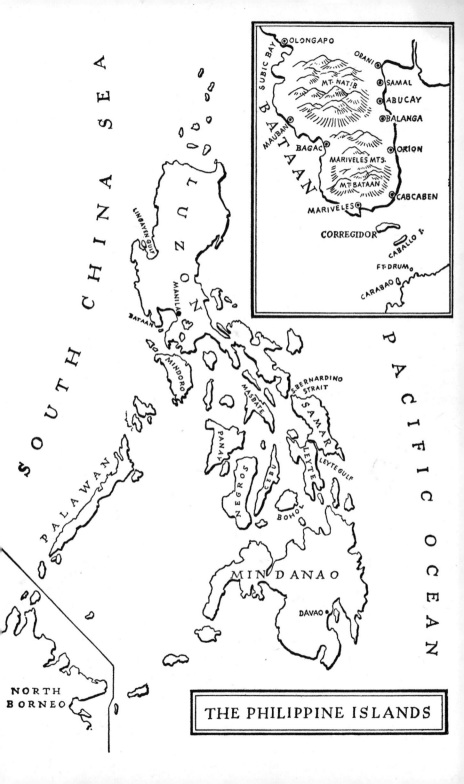

THE PHILIPPINE ISLANDS

cient destroyers, and the six motor torpedo boats, along with a handful of auxiliary ships of various types.

The main Japanese landing force—43,000 Japanese soldiers—began pouring ashore at Lingayen Gulf at five o'clock on the morning of December 22nd. The surf was heavy, and the weather was cold and rainy.

The Japanese assault went well. By the end of the day, against only feeble opposition, Homma's men had captured most of their objectives. Some of the Philippine army troops—revealing their inadequate training and poor equipment—broke and ran as soon as the Japanese approached. The United States' Philippine Scouts, especially the 26th Cavalry, mounted on horses, fought hard, but the Japanese were steadily pushing forward.

General Wainwright asked for permission to withdraw to positions south of the Agno River, some ten miles inland from Lingayen Gulf's southern shore. His thought was that from there he could still launch a successful counterattack. The truth was that unless MacArthur could get strong reinforcements, and get them fast, our forces in the Philippines didn't have a chance.

Since the Japanese had cut our line of communications with the Philippines, men and supplies from the United States would have to travel by way of Australia, a fantastically roundabout route. It was close to hopeless, but even before Homma's main attack, plans were under way to turn Australia into a great forward American base. General George C. Marshall, United States Chief of Staff, had chosen one of MacArthur's former officers to supervise that job. He was a brigadier general named Dwight D. Eisenhower. Eisenhower realized that the men on Luzon couldn't be expected to hold out for long. Still he believed that everything possible should be done, regardless of cost or risk, to reinforce MacArthur.

By December 24th, the picture had grown considerably darker. A second large-scale Japanese landing (although not so big as the main effort) was in progress at Lamon Bay on Luzon's east coast—even closer to Manila than Lingayen Gulf. MacArthur realized that his only chance was to evacuate Manila and order his troops to fall back to the Bataan Peninsula. He would try to defend that craggy thirty-mile-long point of land until help arrived.

It was a last-resort move, and one so drastic that MacArthur had been preparing the Philippine President, Manuel Quezon, for the possibility since December 12th, long before the General believed it would really be necessary. On Christmas Eve, MacArthur's headquarters started to move from Manila to Corregidor, a fortress-island off Bataan's southern tip.

They took President Quezon and the Philippine government's high officials with them. On December 26th, Manila was declared an open city—meaning that it would not be defended, and therefore should not be attacked. The idea was to save as many civilian lives as possible out of Manila's population of 625,-000 men, women, and children.

A huge banner saying "Open City—No Shooting" was hung across the front of the city hall. That night, since there was no longer any point to the blackout, Manila was ablaze with lights. But the roads leading out of town were jammed with Manila residents who were terrified by the idea of Japanese occupation. And they were wise, because for two more days—perhaps because the Japanese didn't know about the open-city declaration—enemy airplanes continued to pour down high explosive on the town. On January 2nd, the Japanese occupied Manila. General Homma had fulfilled the main mission that Imperial General Headquarters had assigned him—except for the fact that MacArthur's small army was in position on Bataan and Corregidor.

Under the difficult circumstances, the withdrawal had gone well, although MacArthur's losses were fairly heavy: their total approached 13,000. Still, not a single big unit had been cut off during the retreat, and MacArthur's lines had usually held when holding was required. As long as Bataan's defenders could stick it out, Homma's victory was incomplete, for the Japanese couldn't use Manila's fine port facilities, or Manila Bay, until Corregidor was in their possession.

The Battle of Bataan began. General Akira Nara was assigned the job of capturing the peninsula. General Homma imagined that our resistance would be slight. That wasn't quite correct. Starting on January 10th, the Japanese moved forward against MacArthur's northernmost defensive line—from Mauban on the west coast, through Mt. Natib in the center, to Abucay on the east. The Philippine army's reaction was immediate and furious. Wherever the Japanese managed to pierce the main battle line, they were thrown back with counterattacks. Homma sent reinforcements and changed commanders. On the second try Major General Naoki Kimura ran the show, and the Japanese pushed ahead faster. By January 26th, MacArthur's men had fallen back to the Bagac-Orion line—a loss of only ten miles or so. But ten miles was a third of Bataan's depth.

The Bataan defenders had been on half-rations for three weeks. A fighting man needs 4,000 calories a day. MacArthur's soldiers had been getting about 2,000; and they were so hungry that the hunt for food began to be all they could think about. The problem posed by unrelenting Japanese attacks seemed, if anything, less important. The final defense line had been reached. No further withdrawal was possible. "With its occupation," MacArthur had radioed Marshall, "all maneuvering possibilities will cease. I intend to fight it out to complete destruction."

For nine more weeks, despite everything the Japanese could do, the Bagac-Orion line was held. General Kimura tried to turn its left flank with amphibious landings at several points along Bataan's southeastern shore, and learned to his regret that the Navy's PT boats, small though they looked, carried a lethal sting.

Speed and maneuverability were the two surprising qualities of the PT boats. Their double mahogany hulls were only 77 feet long, and their three engines, which developed up to 4,200 horsepower, sent them planing through the water at speeds of more than forty miles an hour. They carried very little protective armor, but they were armed with terrific punching power: four 50-caliber machine guns and four 18-inch torpedoes. They were manned by just one officer and a crew of eight. They cost a quarter of a million dollars apiece and, considering the record they made, they were a bargain at the price.

One of Kimura's amphibious forces, heading for Caibobo Point, had the misfortune to run into PT 34, commanded by Lieutenant John D. Bulkeley. Cai-

Lieutenant John D. Bulkeley, commander of PT 34, played an important part in several exciting episodes of World War II.

bobo is five miles south of Bagac. If the surprise Japanese end-run had worked, it might have unhinged the west end of our final Philippine defensive line. But PT 34—helped by the dark night and poor Japanese seamanship—broke up the attack single-handed. Lt. Bulkeley sank one of the troop transports, not realizing that there were other assault vessels all around him. An hour later, PT 34 ran across another landing boat and sank it, as it had the first. Before the Japanese boat went down, Bulkeley boarded it and took two prisoners. By this time, Kimura's landing force had completely lost its bearings, and was split into two groups. Some of the Japanese soldiers came ashore seven miles south of Caibobo. The others landed at Longoskawayan Point, ten miles from where they were supposed to be.

The Japanese did surprise the Americans and the Filipinos, but our confusion wasn't as bad as the enemy's. Some of the Japanese officers, thanks to Bulkeley, never did figure out where they were. Other landings followed, however, which were a serious threat to the Bataan defenses until, as happened in every case, they were beaten back. This "Battle of the Points," as the series of actions was named, was a definite Japanese defeat. They had lost most of two battalions without gaining any advantage.

Meanwhile, on the main Bataan front, the Japanese were not doing any better. They attacked on our right but, after a hard five-day offensive, made only slight progress. We promptly counterattacked and regained all the lost ground.

The Japanese also found that our left was strong. One thousand Japanese infantrymen, pushing through almost impenetrable jungle, advanced along a small river to a point nearly a mile behind our main line of resistance. The foliage was so thick that our artillery did not help us: the shells exploded when they hit the tree tops and were likely to do as much harm to friendly troops as to the enemy. The Japanese were expert at using the jungle for cover and concealment. Their foxholes and gun positions were sometimes practically invisible. Even so, Wainwright's men split this penetration into several pockets, cutting the Japanese off from their own lines. Japanese headquarters tried to drop food and ammunition, but most of the parachute packs fell into American and Filipino hands. Still, the Japanese fought with savage determination. At one point, the Japanese machine guns, expertly emplaced, stopped every attempt to reduce the pocket of resistance.

Lieutenant Willibald C. Bianchi volunteered to lead an infantry platoon, accompanied by one small tank, against the strongpoint. Almost immediately the Lieutenant, who was on foot, got hit in the left hand. He refused first aid. After all, he could still fire his pistol with his right hand. When he got within throwing distance of the first machine gun, Bianchi put it out of action with some well-aimed hand grenades.

Bianchi had hoped that, at the same time, the 37-millimeter gun on the tank would be wiping out the second Japanese machine gun. That wasn't working out. The tank's gun wouldn't depress far enough to fire toward the ground. Bianchi saw the solution: the tank also carried a mounted machine gun, designed to give it anti-aircraft protection. It could do the job.

But before Bianchi could act, two more Japanese bullets hit him, wounding him in the chest. By some miracle, even so, Bianchi found the strength to scramble onto the tank, climb to the anti-aircraft gun, swing its muzzle down, and pour a stream of lead into the second Japanese position.

A fourth Japanese bullet hit Bianchi, sending him spinning off the tank. But, as he learned later, his shots had wiped out the second machine gun. Bianchi was evacuated to the hospital, and in just a month he was well enough to return to his outfit. For his bravery, he was awarded America's highest military decoration, the Congressional Medal of Honor.

Wainwright's men restored the battle line on our left. By the end of the first week in February, General Homma had to face the fact that he did not have strength to break the Philippine-American defenses. Some of his units had been wiped out. His casualties were so great that, in Homma's estimation, only three of his battalions could be called effective fighting outfits.

Homma ordered his troops to fall back, and he asked Tokyo to send him reinforcements. On our side, morale was high. The tragedy was that no help was coming for Wainwright's tired men. They were going to have to make do with what they had—and they had far too little of everything.

In Washington, at about this time, the high command, fearing that Bataan was doomed to fall, decided that MacArthur couldn't be allowed to fall into Japanese hands. He had to be rescued, despite any objections he might raise, to lead other forces in the battles yet to come.

General Marshall first opened the delicate question by asking MacArthur, in a cable, what plans he had for evacuating his wife and his young son, who were with the General on Corregidor. Then, on February 22nd, President Roosevelt ordered MacArthur to leave Corregidor as quickly as possible. The General was to proceed to Mindanao, and from there to Australia where he was to take command of the entire Southwest Pacific area.

When the President's orders reached Corregidor, General MacArthur drafted a blunt note refusing to accept them. The President is the commander-in-chief, and if MacArthur had actually refused to obey orders—as his staff quickly reminded him—he would have faced a court-martial.

Finally MacArthur wrote a new message, accepting, and asking only that he be allowed to pick the right psychological time to leave. "These people are depending upon me . . ." MacArthur wrote, "and any idea that might develop in their minds that I was being withdrawn for any other purpose than to bring them immediate relief could not be explained. . . ."

On March 12th, just as it was getting dark, four PT boats, under Lieutenant Bulkeley's tactical command, took General MacArthur, his wife, his son, and the eighteen other members of the party, off Corregidor. They worked their way cautiously through the defensive mine fields that we had laid down at the entrance to the harbor, and then raced through the night, Mindanao bound.

Three days earlier MacArthur had spoken to Wainwright, who was to command the troops on Bataan. MacArthur had promised to "come back as soon as I can with as much as I can."

"Be sure to give him [the enemy] everything you've got with your artillery," MacArthur said. "That's the best arm you have."

Wainwright said he'd do everything he could, and he promised he'd still be on Bataan when MacArthur returned—a promise he couldn't keep.

By this time Wainwright's soldiers were down to quarter-rations. Their uniforms were in rags and tatters. Many of them had no shoes. Men were dropping with malaria, dysentery, and simple starvation.

By the end of March, scarcely any of Bataan's defenders were still optimistic enough to think that reinforcements and supplies would actually reach them.

Most of them suspected that death or capture—it was hard to decide which was preferable—was the choice they faced.

You might think that under these circumstances our GI's would have grown despondent and bitter. But, as usual, they made grim jokes about their fate.

Many of them would never know how frantically Marshall in Washington, and his subordinates between there and Australia, were trying to get food, medicine, and ammunition to Bataan. The Japanese blockade was discouragingly effective. There were very few ships around that had any hope of smuggling a cargo through it. The War Department had a million dollars to spend on blockade-running, but more than money was required. A few ships did make the dangerous run, but all told they delivered less than one thousand tons of supplies to Corregidor and Bataan. Since more than 100,000 soldiers and civilians were waiting for them, that wasn't much. General Marshall tried everything. Some old destroyers that had been converted into cargo ships were rushed from New Orleans, Louisiana, through the Panama Canal, but the effort was too late. A few submarines got through successfully. A few small planes managed to sneak into Bataan at night. But the relief that planes and submarines could carry, while tremendously appreciated, was pitifully small.

Japanese troops celebrate their victory on Bataan.

On Friday, April 3rd, General Homma renewed his attack, with a tremendous air and artillery bombardment. The Japanese had been reinforced, regrouped, and rested. Their supplies were excellent. It scarely mattered how bravely the Americans and Filipinos fought; they were overwhelmed. On the sixth of April, Wainwright's men attempted to counterattack, and spent their last energies on that gallant effort. On the seventh and eighth, the Bataan defenses disintegrated and collapsed. On the ninth, the 78,000 men who were left on Bataan surrendered.

What happened to these men was not known for three years, when the War and Navy Departments released the carefully documented, sickening story of the "March of Death" from Bataan to prison camp at San Fernando, sixty-five miles north of the surrender point. There are international rules governing the treatment of captured soldiers. The Japanese did worse than break every rule in the book: their behavior was inhuman. A sixty-five-mile march is an ordeal under the best circumstances, but the Japanese guards allowed the Americans and Filipinos practically no food or water, and seemed to enjoy torturing their helpless prisoners. They beheaded American soldiers who had Japanese money among their possessions, on the false theory that it must have been stolen from dead Japanese soldiers. Anyone too sick or exhausted to keep up with the march was shot, and the stronger prisoners were not allowed to help the weak. By the time the gruesome march was over, some 5,000 American prisoners had been murdered, and the Filipino dead outnumbered the American total by far.

Corregidor and its sister forts across Manila Bay were still in American hands. But Corregidor couldn't hope to hold out long after the Japanese started firing artillery from the southern tip of Bataan, just two miles away. The shelling began on the ninth of April. and it never really stopped. The Japanese kept adding more and more guns to the barrage until they had a hundred pieces—from 75-millimeter to 240-millimeter —trained on Corregidor. They could fire almost incessantly. On rare occasions when their guns weren't in action, the Japanese attacked Corregidor from the air. The pounding went on for twenty-seven days.

About the only safe place on the whole island was Malinta Tunnel, under Malinta Hill. This was a large network of reinforced concrete passageways big enough to shelter a headquarters, a hospital, various shops, and a huge underground storehouse. It was extremely crowded, and it became almost unbearable when a Japanese bomb damaged the power plant which supplied it with fresh air and electricity. But, above all, the trouble with Corregidor was a water shortage. The dry season was at hand, and rain water was the island's main reliance. By May, there was only enough water to last for one more week.

On May 5th, around midnight, after nearly a month's preparatory bombardment, the Japanese began landing on Corregidor, which had been turned into a desolate, shell-cratered no man's land. There was no hope that the Americans and Filipinos—although there were almost 12,000 of them—could check the efficient landing operation. General Wainwright surrendered Corregidor and called on all the troops in the Philippines—for isolated forces were still fighting in some places, like the islands of Panay, Cebu, and Mindanao—to lay down their arms.

The victory which Homma had expected to win by the middle of February had taken more than twice as long as the Japanese schedule allowed. (Homma was in disgrace on that account. He was relieved of his command and returned to Tokyo, where he sat out the rest of the war.)

It was a crushing defeat for the United States, but the Philippines' defenders, at terrible cost, had not failed entirely. They had kept resistance alive for six months. They had forced the Japanese to pay heavily in men and planes for ground that had only a secondary rating in their overall plan for conquest. Before the Philippine army gave up, the Japanese had swept over Southeast Asia, through the Solomons, and eastward as far as the Gilbert Islands. Everywhere else, the Japanese had succeeded so easily that, without Bataan and Corregidor as proof of what brave men could do, the world might have thought that Japan's military strength was invincible.

That was far from true, but the fallacy had to be proved. MacArthur's men had provided the first installment on that proof.

3

Guadalcanal: The Tide Turns

By May, 1942, the Japanese had come close to winning everything Tojo wanted.

They had captured the Netherlands East Indies: Sumatra, Borneo, Java, Celebes, Amboina, Bali, and Timor.

They had seized Rabaul on New Britain, one of the finest natural harbors in the Pacific, and had developed it into a major base. They had landed at Lae and Salamaua on the coast of Northeast New Guinea; and they were working their way, island by island, southeast through the Solomon Islands toward Tulagi and Guadalcanal.

They had invaded Burma, captured Rangoon—Burma's main port—and had occupied the Andaman Islands in the Bay of Bengal, off Burma's west coast.

Japan was triumphant. There was just one annoying failure, from Tojo's point of view: the United States, though heartsick over all she and her allies had lost, was not discouraged.

On the contrary, we had reinforced the Hawaiian Islands, and our supply line to Australia—6,000 dangerous miles long—was growing stronger day by day. MacArthur, in his Australian headquarters, was organizing that country's defenses. All Allied plans depended on Australia's safety, for there was no other place in the South Pacific that could serve so well as a military base.

MacArthur worried about the Japanese on New Britain, New Guinea, and Timor, as well as in the Solomons. They were much too close to Australia, and to the Allied shipping lanes.

Here and there United States forces had enjoyed small victories. These hadn't stopped the wave of Japanese success, or even slowed it down, but they had done wonders for American morale. In February and March, small carrier task forces from Hawaii had dealt the Japanese a few stinging counterpunches, proving how unlucky the Japanese had been to miss our carriers when they bombed Pearl Harbor.

Vice Admiral William F. Halsey, Jr.—known to his men as "Fighting Bill," "Wild Bill," or "Bull" Halsey—led the *Enterprise,* three cruisers, and six destroyers in a daring raid against Wotje in the Marshall Islands, sinking seven enemy ships in the harbor and pounding the Japanese fortifications. At the same time Rear Admiral Frank Jack Fletcher with the *Yorktown,* two cruisers, and four destroyers was raising havoc in other parts of the Marshalls. Halsey also struck with lightning surprise at Wake Island, and at Marcus Island, less than a thousand miles from Yokohama, and gave a good working-over to the Japanese airfields, hangars, and anti-aircraft batteries.

A similar carrier task force, commanded by Vice Admiral Wilson Brown, had sailed into the Solomons soon after the Japanese captured Rabaul, hoping to smash some part of that fine base. The strike was called off because two patrol planes spotted Brown's approaching force, and the necessary element of surprise was therefore lost.

The same afternoon, two waves of Japanese planes attacked our retreating task force. The first wave was beaten off, but half an hour later, the second V-formation of nine Japanese planes arrived. By this time, all but two of the *Lexington*'s fighter planes were on the deck, refueling. The two Americans attacked the Japanese formation. One of the pilots,

Lt. Edward "Butch" O'Hare of St. Louis, Missouri, soon realized that his partner's guns had jammed. O'Hare took on all nine of the Japanese planes by himself. He flew straight at the formation five separate times, sticking with his attack even after the bombers had flown into the task force's anti-aircraft fire. The whole skirmish lasted four minutes, and the *Lexington* and all her airplanes were safe. When O'Hare's score was added up it came to five bombers destroyed, and a sixth so badly crippled that it was presumed lost.

President Roosevelt, awarding O'Hare the Medal of Honor, called it "the most daring single action in the history of combat aviation."

Then, on April 18th—the 167th anniversary of Paul Revere's ride—sixteen medium bombers (B-25's), led by Lieutenant Colonel James H. Doolittle, gave the Japanese cities, Yokohama, Nagoya, Kobe, Tokyo, and Osaka, a nerve-wracking foretaste of air raids to come. Doolittle's planes took off from carriers, although the B-25 was designed to operate from land. (Nothing its size had ever taken off from a ship before, except experimentally.) The carrier *Hornet* joined the *Enterprise* in a task force commanded by Halsey which sailed to within 700 miles of Japan—a daring feat in itself, because land-based Japanese planes, if they had found it, might have given Halsey's ships a bad beating.

Aboard the Hornet, pilots led by Colonel Doolittle start the engines of their B-25's.

Doolittle's planes delivered their bombs. Then, according to plan, the B-25's headed for the China coast, where, unable to reach their assigned landing fields, they crash-landed or their crews bailed out. (Except for one plane, which crash-landed at Vladivostok, a Soviet Union seaport.) The Japanese, who had thought their home islands were safely beyond bombing range, were aghast. The damage to their cities was not especially great, but the Doolittle raid was a blow to Japanese morale, and it helped cause a complete—and mistaken—change in Japanese strategy.

When they realized that our bombers could reach Japan, and in view of the ease with which they had been winning nearly everywhere, the Japanese decided to launch a major expedition against Midway. They hoped to draw the surviving ships of the United States Pacific Fleet into battle and destroy them. Instead of consolidating what they had, the Japanese felt they needed a little bit more.

This meant that Japan had to split her powerful force of six aircraft carriers. Two of them—the *Shokaku* and the *Zuikaku*—were needed to support the Japanese army drives toward Port Moresby on New Guinea, and Tulagi in the Solomons. The other four were assigned to the Midway attacks.

That was a bad mistake: it gave the United States Navy a chance to win two important sea battles.

Two of our four carriers, the *Yorktown* and the *Lexington,* were in the Coral Sea, which lies between Australia and New Guinea. The Allies simply could not afford to let the Japanese take Port Moresby if they could possibly prevent it. Japanese planes, based on Port Moresby, could have made northern Australia practically unusable.

On May 7th, when the Japanese moved toward Port Moresby, two American carrier task forces moved in to intercept their invasion fleet. A furious sea and air battle raged for thirty hours.

We paid a staggeringly high price for a strategic victory. The *Lexington* was sunk. The *Yorktown* was damaged, and two smaller warships were sunk.

Five hundred and forty-three of our men were casualties.

Our losses were considerably higher than the Japanese losses, although both their carriers were damaged—the *Shokaku* so badly that it was months before she would return to action.

But the Allies counted the Battle of the Coral Sea as a victory because Port Moresby had been saved. Japan's invasion force was stopped in its tracks. The troop transports were forced to turn around and head back for Rabaul. At Imperial General Headquarters, in Tokyo, the Japanese thought they could remount the Port Moresby attack within a couple of months. The fact was that they would never get there.

The Battle of Midway, in June, was an unqualified American victory. Admiral Chester W. Nimitz, who had taken command of the Pacific Fleet not long after Pearl Harbor, knew that the Japanese were planning something big, for the United States had broken the secret Japanese code and had intercepted enough radio messages to figure out that Midway was Admiral Yamamoto's objective.

The Japanese had assembled a tremendous attacking force. There were four big carriers (*Kaga, Akagi, Hiryu* and *Soryu*), seven battleships, and a large assortment of cruisers, light cruisers, and destroyers. Yamamoto was confident of a quick, overwhelming success. And as soon as the Japanese had Midway well in hand,

Yamamoto's fleet was expected to assist in the seizure of New Caledonia, Fiji, Samoa—and, finally, return to the matter of Port Moresby.

Our defensive strength, while it was practically everything we had, couldn't quite match Japan's forces, but there were more United States ships defending Midway than Yamamoto realized. The Japanese hoped that they had sunk the *Yorktown* in the Coral Sea. But she had only been damaged, and now, patched up, was eager for revenge. We had no battleships at all, but there were seven heavy cruisers and fourteen destroyers on hand. And some 200 miles north of Midway, ready for action, lay the *Enterprise,* the *Hornet,* and the *Yorktown.*

On the morning of June 4th, Japanese carrier-based planes opened the assault on Midway with a powerful bombardment—preparation for the landings that were supposed to follow. While the Japanese planes were refueling and rearming, dive-bomber squadrons from the *Enterprise* and the *Yorktown* flashed down out of the skies upon the *Akagi,* the *Kaga,* and the *Soryu,* which were closely bunched. In a matter of minutes, all three carriers were fatally damaged. The *Kaga* and the *Soryu* went down late in the afternoon. Uncontrollable fires raged through the *Akagi,* and she was finally sunk by a Japanese destroyer.

The *Hiryu,* which had been a considerable distance ahead of the others, and was supported by two battleships, knocked out the *Yorktown.* But dive bombers from the *Hornet* and the *Enterprise* promptly evened that score: they hit the *Hiryu,* starting a fire which blazed all through the night. The next morning, a Japanese destroyer took off the last of the *Hiryu's* crew and sank the derelict with a spread of torpedoes.

It was an almost incredible victory for the United States. At the cost of a carrier, a destroyer, 150 planes, and 300 men, the Pacific Fleet had broken the back of Japan's long-range striking power. From that day on, Japanese ships scarcely ventured beyond the air protection of land-based planes. Midway was safe. The attacks against New Caledonia, Fiji, and Samoa had to be abandoned. On the ocean front, Japan was on the defensive.

Yamamoto broke off the engagement, and swung north and west, with United States naval units in pursuit.

In the new kind of naval fighting that had developed —in which the carrier task force, instead of the line of battleships, was all important—the United States Navy had done the near impossible. In less than six months, by daring use of our four carriers, the *Lexington,* the *Yorktown,* the *Enterprise,* and the *Hornet,* we had almost made up for our Pearl Harbor disaster.

No one quite realized it, but Tojo's mad dream had started to become a Japanese nightmare. Japan's war leaders had gambled everything on quick victory. Their country lacked the productive power to fight a long war against the United States. Japan could not easily replace the ships she had lost at Coral Sea and Midway. Her armed forces were engaged over such a tremendous area that she didn't have quite enough cargo ships to supply the far-flung outposts of Tojo's "defensive perimeter." And she had still fewer cargo ships after American submarines began sinking them.

Of course the United States was helping to fight another war on the other side of the globe. By the summer of 1942, we were getting ready to land forces on the northern coast of Africa. But America's tremendous industrial capacity was just getting into high gear. Our population then was only 135,000,000, and before victory was won 13,000,000 of our young men and women were going to enter the United States armed forces. But there were 60,000,000 Americans at home working to turn out the thousand and one things required to wage war.

Aircraft carriers—to take one example—illustrated the difference. Japan had trouble building carriers to replace the four she had lost. On the other hand, as soon as we had realized the value of the carrier task force and had pushed our shipyards to their top capacity, we could construct six *Essex*-class carriers a year. That was the biggest size, with an 888-foot flight deck, displacing 25,000 tons. These *Essex*-class carriers were in addition to the fast, wide-ranging *Independence*-class carriers (11,000 tons) we could build at the same time, as well as countless conversions of tanker or cargo-ship hulls into "baby flat-tops."

There was one temporary consolation for the Japanese. During the Battle of Midway—partly as an unsuccessful diversion to draw off American strength—they had bombed the United States naval and air base at Dutch Harbor, Unalaska, in the Aleutian Islands, and landed occupation forces on Attu and Kiska. The weather in the Aleutians is so bad that as military bases neither island was especially useful. Yet, in Japanese hands, they were good observation posts; and, if the Japanese ever intended to move against Dutch Harbor, Kiska was a likely jumping-off point. The United States watched carefully, from then on, to make sure that the Japanese were not building up strength on either island.

By mid-summer, MacArthur was itching to take the offensive. He had improved Port Moresby as a base, and he wanted to strike from there across New Guinea to Rabaul, the Japanese stronghold. Everyone agreed that Rabaul was, for the time being, our key target. But in Washington our Joint Chiefs, worried about the supply lines to Australia, felt that first the Allies had to keep the Japanese from advancing any farther into the southeast Solomons.

The Japanese, on the other hand, were more eager than ever to capture Port Moresby. Before the Allies made any move, the enemy landed at Buna, on the northern coast of the Papuan Peninsula, just one hundred air miles from Port Moresby.

From a soldier's viewpoint, Papua is impossible, a jungle where ten inches of rain may fall in a single day. The Owen-Stanley Mountains run down the peninsula. Some of their peaks are 13,000 feet high. A man could freeze in the mountains at night after having sweltered in the coastal jungle all day. Since the Japanese had been unable to reach Port Moresby by sea, they now planned to march across the mountains from Buna, over a rugged trail called the Kokoda "road"—built for pack mules rather than jeeps and guarded by Australian troops.

The Australians were amazed when the Japanese, in considerable strength, pushed in the direction of Kokoda. Within a few days the Japanese had covered more than half the distance to Port Moresby. The

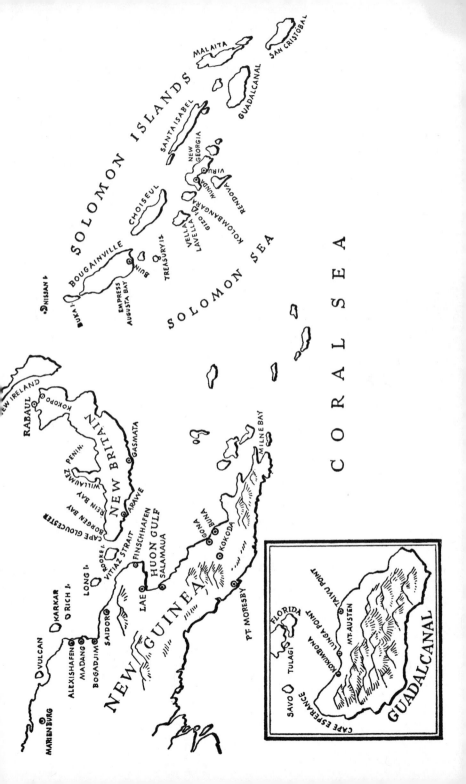

Japanese commander thought that all he needed was some coördinated naval support to shell Port Moresby from the sea while he pushed on from the land side.

But just at the critical time—the first week in August—the United States was also on the offensive in the southeast Solomons, at Tulagi and Guadalcanal. For the moment the Japanese navy had its hands full, and the job of supporting the Port Moresby thrust had to be postponed.

We had discovered that the Japanese were building an airstrip at Lunga Point on Guadalcanal. Land-based planes, operating from there, could be a menace to our supply ships. Little Tulagi Island, almost directly north of Lunga Point, was also very much in our minds because it guarded the best sheltered anchorage for miles around—a fine natural base for Japanese warships and seaplanes.

At daybreak on August 7th, the United States 1st Marine Division (reinforced) went ashore at both places —our first offensive action on the ground.

The Japanese were completely surprised. Bad weather had interfered with their air reconnaissance and, besides, Japanese headquarters didn't think we were ready to try a full-scale amphibious assault.

There was something to the Japanese opinion. We were not entirely ready. Our landings were a daring shoestring operation. We had the strength to put the marines ashore—as long as we achieved surprise. But just how we could keep them on Tulagi and Guadalcanal wasn't quite clear.

Major General Alexander A. Vandegrift had divided his force of about 19,000 men into several combat groups. His main strength—10,000 marines—landed on Guadalcanal, which he considered by far the tougher objective. Another 6,000 headed for Tulagi, making four separate landings, including two on Florida Island, in order to protect their flanks.

The landings had very strong naval support. There were planes from three carriers—the *Saratoga,* the *Enterprise,* and the *Wasp,* newly arrived in the combat area—and a powerful fleet of cruisers and destroyers guarding the troop transports as well as providing prelanding bombardment of the assault beaches.

But it was far too dangerous for this great armada to stand by after the landing. The Navy would have to withdraw, leaving the marines on their own.

Getting ashore proved absurdly easy. There were fewer Japanese on Guadalcanal than our intelligence had estimated, and many were not combat soldiers, but laborers working on the airstrip. As the marines approached the beach, all but a few of these Japanese faded back into the jungle, abandoning weapons and equipment. The Tulagi landings also went smoothly, but when the Marine Raiders were within a mile or so

American troops on Guadalcanal met heavy Japanese resistance. Here a marine gun crew blasts away at an enemy position.

of their final objective, Hill 281, they were halted by Japanese rifles and machine-gun fire. That first night ashore, our Tulagi force was tested by four Japanese counterattacks. As they had already proved in other battles, Japanese infantrymen were expert night fighters. For a time, one company of marines was cut off from the rest of the battalion. But they held their ground. By dawn, the Japanese thrusts had been repelled. During the day the marines put an end to organized resistance on Tulagi.

Unorganized resistance, however, was another matter. Small groups of Japanese soldiers—and in some cases individual men—were hiding in scattered caves, dugouts, and bunkers. They were determined to resist to the death. They had been taught, like all Japanese soldiers for some 1600 years, that dying in battle was their religious-patriotic duty—the code of *Bushido,* as it was called.

Those who did not believe in it realized that their being taken prisoner would disgrace their families as well as themselves. And many Japanese soldiers thought the Americans would torture prisoners to death—as, indeed, the Japanese were torturing the American survivors of Bataan and Corregidor.

For days after Tulagi was in American hands, the marines were forced to blast fanatic Japanese out of their hideouts—a dangerous, slow, and horrible job. A Marine Corps interpreter was sent to one cave, hoping to persuade a trapped Japanese officer to give up. The officer's only answer was to throw a hand grenade at the interpreter.

Some Japanese committed suicide, but for those who held out their dugouts were small fortresses. The best way of taking them—a nerve-wracking method which resulted in scores of marine casualties—was to push dynamite into the entrance tunnel. After the explosion, with luck, the marines could usually charge in and finish off the survivors in hand-to-hand combat. Of the entire Japanese force on Tulagi, we took only one prisoner. And he really didn't count. At the moment he surrendered, he was dazed by the blast of a

mortar shell and didn't quite know what he was doing.

We knew that the Tulagi success and the quick
advance on Guadalcanal were the products of surprise. The marines had caught the Japanese off guard.
It was unlikely that the Japanese meant to give up
their air-sea bases without a major fight.

As soon as Japanese headquarters heard what had
happened, it started a powerful naval task force moving
toward Guadalcanal: five heavy cruisers, two light
cruisers, and a destroyer.

The marines' supporting warships had not yet left
the narrow waters between Guadalcanal and Florida
Island—"The Slot," as it had been nicknamed—despite the danger of getting caught there without room
enough to maneuver.

On the night of August 8, 1942, Vice Admiral Gun-
ichi Mikawa's task force managed to slip past two of
our destroyers on patrol duty at the mouth of The
Slot. Our invasion fleet didn't know the Japanese
were coming until, at half past one in the morning,
their torpedoes flashed from their tubes and began to
score deadly hits. Four cruisers were sunk or fatally
damaged: the *Vincennes,* the *Quincy,* the *Astoria,*
and Australia's *Canberra.* The cruiser *Chicago* had
part of her bow blown off. The destroyer *Ralph Talbot*
was hit.

Not far beyond these ships lay the fleet of troop transport and supply ships. It was just lucky that the Japanese called off their attack before they found them. American losses might have been worse.

Our warships withdrew from The Slot—all that could still do so—taking the transports with them. But the marines' supply ships were only partially unloaded, and there were still quite a few soldiers on board the transports who were waiting to be ferried ashore. The Navy's withdrawal left Vandegrift's men isolated. They lacked some pieces of important equipment. Their food supplies were limited. They had only four days' worth of ammunition—in case the fighting got really heavy.

The Guadalcanal airstrip—which the marines hurriedly lengthened and renamed Henderson Field— became more important than ever. Supplies in limited quantities could be delivered by air. Other materiel was brought in by overage destroyers, converted into transports, which boldly ran into The Slot at night and unloaded before the Japanese could spot them.

But the enemy's planes and warships kept the Guadalcanal beachhead under continual attack. They bombed and shelled the marines' positions night and day. And, as expected, in ten days' time, a 1,000-man Japanese force landed twenty miles east of Henderson Field, near Taivu Point. Four thousand additional

Japanese soldiers were on the way. Three weeks later, another Japanese force landed only eleven miles west of Henderson Field. It contained another 1,000 men.

The Japanese plan was to attack the marines' small beachhead around the airstrip from all three sides at once. At the same time, it would be shelled from the sea and bombed from the air.

Vandegrift had dug in. He knew that the marines' toe hold was precarious. His best news had been the arrival of 31 Marine fighter planes and dive bombers which had flown into Henderson Field—a start toward the air support he needed badly. South of Henderson Field, on a long, low ridge that extended inland for about a thousand yards, Vandegrift posted eight companies of the Raider and Parachute battalions. They guarded the back door to the beachhead. Unless it was properly defended this ridge offered the Japanese a path into the beachhead. It was about to earn the name it has had ever since: Bloody Ridge.

General Kiyotake Kawaguchi opened his attack on the evening of September 12th. The first alarm came when Colonel Merritt A. Edson, commanding the 1st Raider Battalion, walked down Bloody Ridge with some of his staff, discussing the position. They drew small-arms fire from the jungle to the south. Edson's men dug in on the southernmost knoll of the Ridge, planning to attack the next morning. That same night

An encampment on the Guadalcanal front line has a respite from battle.

Colonel Merritt A. Edson, commander of the 1st Raider Battalion, holds a meeting of his staff.

a Japanese cruiser and three Japanese destroyers rushed through The Slot, firing on Henderson Field.

The marines were not sure just how strong the Japanese were—or what they intended.

Edson's attack jumped off at daybreak. His men meant to find out who had been shooting at the Colonel, and it didn't take long to get an answer. The jungle contained Kawaguchi's main force, better than two battalions strong, and reinforced by engineers, artillery, and assorted special troops. For the sake of surprise, Kawaguchi had ordered his men to cut a trail over the jungle-covered ridges almost all the way from the Taivu Point area—nearly twenty miles of strenuous road-building at the rate of two miles a day. The Japanese had achieved their surprise, but they paid heavily for the advantage. Some of Kawaguchi's men reached the battlefield in a state of semi-exhaustion.

Even so, as Edson's marines quickly saw, the Japanese force was very strong. The Colonel ordered a tactical withdrawal. He pulled back up the Ridge, shortening the marines' line. A dangerously wide stretch of ground had to be held by far too few men.

It looked as if the night of the 13th was going to be worse than the 12th had been. Henderson Field had been taking a severe daylight pounding from the air, and the Marine scouting planes had discovered seven

Japanese destroyers steaming into The Slot, headed for Lunga Point.

As the sky darkened, Edson's men worked hard to improve their foxholes. "Washing-Machine Charlie" —as the marines called a twin-engined Japanese bomber that hit Guadalcanal almost every night on regular schedule—flew over and dropped a scattering of high explosive. At nine o'clock, an aerial flare hung in the sky over Henderson Field. It was an aiming point for the gunners on the Japanese destroyers. They opened fire and began pouring shells into the Marine beachhead. At the same moment, Kawaguchi's two battalions hit hard against Edson's new positions slightly to the south of the middle of the Ridge.

One aggressive Japanese column found an opening between two of Edson's companies, and swarmed into the gap. A battalion of 105-millimeter howitzers was supporting the marines. Edson ordered the curtain of falling shells brought closer and closer to his own position, but the Japanese kept coming. They occupied some of the marines' outermost foxholes, and began pouring mortar shells on top of the Ridge.

Just before midnight, the main Japanese power shifted from the right to the left side of Edson's line, where the Parachute companies were dug in. Kawaguchi's men fired smoke shells. When the smoke hung over the Ridge in a cloud, they yelled, in English, "Gas attack! Gas attack!" It wasn't gas at all, just smoke. Before the marines caught on to the trick, Japanese infantrymen charged out of the jungle and forced the parachutists to give ground. The right side of Edson's line, where the casualties had been frightful, was now exposed. Edson ordered his whole line to pull back onto the knoll—the last good position south of the airstrip. He meant to fight there to the last man.

All night the bloody struggle raged on. Kawaguchi's infantrymen hurled themselves at the knoll in at least a dozen savage assaults. The marines could not be budged.

By daylight, Bloody Ridge was strewn with both American and Japanese casualties, but Lunga Point and Henderson Field were still safely in Marine hands. Three American planes took off from the airstrip, and drove Kawaguchi's men back into the jungle.

More than six hundred dead Japanese were counted on the battlefield. As an effective fighting unit, Kawaguchi's battalions were completely spent. The marines would never forget the Battle of Bloody Ridge—or Edson's Ridge, as some of them called it—and yet it was just a sample of the fighting that continued on Guadalcanal for five more months.

In mid-October, one month later, the Japanese tried almost the same scheme—but on a much larger scale. A fleet of Japanese battleships, cruisers, and destroyers swept down The Slot, stood off Lunga Point, and pounded Henderson Field with the greatest volume of naval gunfire so far. Japanese planes added to the bombardment. On top of all that, the Japanese had landed medium artillery—150-millimeter howitzers—in the Kokumbona area. They lobbed their high-explosive shells into the beachhead with dreadful accuracy.

Henderson Field was temporarily knocked out. Half of the ninety planes that had been in operating shape a day earlier were too badly damaged to fly. The marines' makeshift collection of patched-up planes were known as "The Cactus Air Force," and they had been through so much already that they no longer knew when they were licked. While repairs were still being made, some of the surviving aircraft, dodging shell craters, managed to bounce into the air from an auxiliary fighter airstrip and attack the enemy's approaching ground troops. They sank two big Japanese transports. They set three others on fire, and the Japanese were forced to run them ashore to prevent their sinking.

General Haruyoshi Hyakutake, who succeeded General Kawaguchi, had a force of 20,000 men. Instead of profiting from Kawaguchi's mistakes, Hyakutake, who was overconfident, repeated them. The Japanese got as far as Bloody Ridge, and no farther. The battle was furious, but the marines held their ground. When the smoke cleared, Hyakutake's divisions, like Kawaguchi's battalions before them, had been cut to ribbons.

The Japanese high command was still unwilling to admit that taking Lunga Point from the 1st Marine Division was more than the Emperor's forces could manage. A third great effort was scheduled for November. This time brilliant action by the United States Navy broke the momentum of the Japanese attack. A series of sea battles lasting three days left the Japanese invasion fleet in complete confusion, with several of its ships resting on the bottom of the sea.

One engagement in this series involved a task force —five United States cruisers and eight destroyers— commanded by Rear Admiral Daniel J. Callaghan. Our ships had just finished convoying some welcome reinforcements to Guadalcanal. Word came that a tremendous Japanese armada was steadily steaming toward The Slot, and Callaghan took his thirteen ships, in single file, to meet them. It was Friday, November 13th. The night was inky black, without even a star showing in the sky. At 1:24 A.M. our search radar picked up two groups of enemy ships. Without knowing exactly how many they were, Callaghan changed course and headed straight for them. He sailed into the middle of the Japanese formation.

There were fourteen Japanese warships, including two battleships, a cruiser, and eleven destroyers. It meant that they could throw at least three times as much steel as we could, and, to make matters ever so much worse, the Japanese were on both sides of Callaghan's comparatively weak column.

For the moment, the American task force had an advantage; the Japanese didn't realize that Callaghan was there.

Just before Callaghan's ships opened fire, however, the Japanese searchlights came on. Our task force was caught in a blaze of light from two directions. Seconds later, the Japanese shells started screaming down those paths of light.

The Admiral's order was a model of cool thinking. "Odd ships fire to starboard, even to port!"

They did just that, and with remarkable success, considering the heavy odds against the smaller United States force.

For fifteen minutes a fantastic free-for-all gunnery battle took place. Torpedoes streaked in every direction. Geysers of water flashed into the air. The noise made by the booming of the guns was worse than thunder. All but one of Callaghan's ships were hit. More important, the Japanese fleet, astonished by the action, turned around and sailed away. Callaghan's mission was to stop the Japanese fleet, no matter what

U. S. S. R.
MONGOLIA
CHINA
VLADIVOSTOK
SAKHALIN I.
KOREA
JAPAN
TOKYO
BURMA
INDOCHINA
THAILAND
HAINAN
FORMOSA
OKINAWA
IWO JIMA
MARCUS
WAKE
MALAY PENINSULA
PHILIPPINE IS.
SAIPAN
GUAM
MARSHALL
ENIWETOK
ULITHI
PALAU
PULAP
TRUK
PONAPE
JALUIT
CAROLINE ISLANDS
SUMATRA
SINGAPORE
BORNEO
CELEBES
GILBERT IS
NEW GUINEA
INDONESIA
SOLOMON IS.
JAVA
TIMOR
STA·CRUZ
CORAL SEA
NEW HEBRIDES
NEW CALEDONIA
AUSTRALIA
TASMANIA

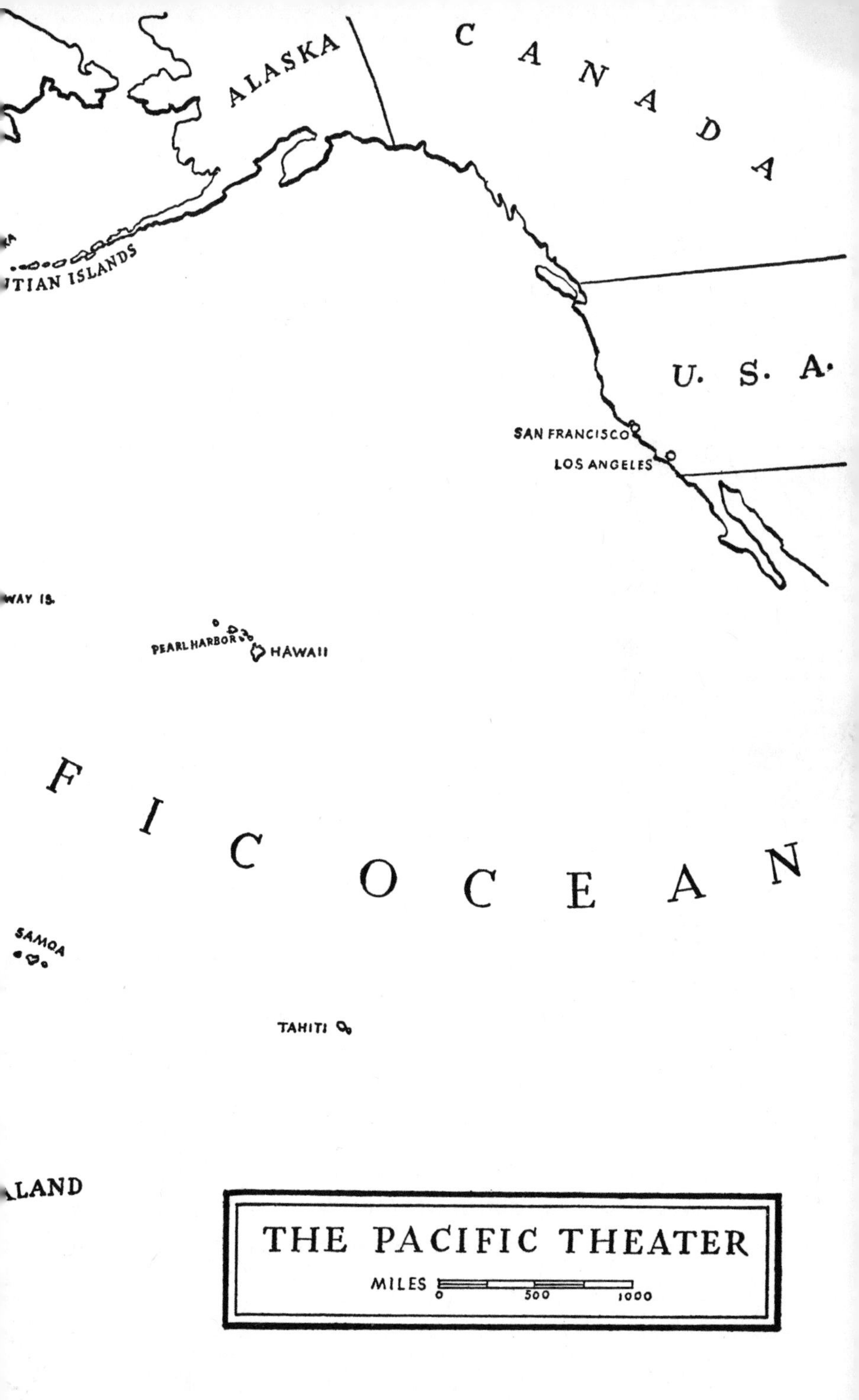

ALASKA

CANADA

UTIAN ISLANDS

U. S. A.

SAN FRANCISCO

LOS ANGELES

WAY IS.

PEARL HARBOR   HAWAII

F I C   O C E A N

SAMOA

TAHITI

LAND

THE PACIFIC THEATER

MILES

0   500   1000

the cost. His mission was accomplished. The cost included Callaghan's life. An enemy salvo had smashed the bridge of his flagship, the *San Francisco*, and the Admiral was dead. But not one shell fell on Henderson Field that night.

In December, General Vandegrift and the 1st Marine Division, worn out after four months of almost non-stop fighting, got relief. The Division's casualties amounted to 605 officers and men killed in action, 76 who had died of wounds, or were missing and presumed dead, and 1,278 wounded. Malaria and other tropical diseases had been as dangerous as the Japanese. Almost 9,000 of the marines had been hospitalized at one time or another, though out of necessity front-line troops weren't even allowed light duty unless their fever was higher than 103 degrees.

Major General Alexander M. Patch, commanding a corps made up of the Americal Division, the 25th Infantry, and the 2nd Marine Division, took over from the 1st Marines. Finally we were strong enough to take the offensive, and to drive the Japanese completely off Guadalcanal. There were some 20,000 Japanese soldiers scattered here and there, prepared to fight for every machine-gun nest. Luckily, we did not have to beat them man by man. By January, the Japanese were having serious difficulties on New Guinea. They decided to pull out of Guadalcanal and establish new positions in the Solomons, closer to their base, Rabaul.

General Patch had no way of knowing this. He drove toward Cape Esperance, thinking the Japanese might try to hold there, waiting for reinforcements. But the Japanese weren't holding; they were getting out. By February 8, 1943, in a remarkable evacuation, using submarines, destroyers, and every fast boat they could find, the Japanese managed to rescue all their high-ranking officers and most of their men.

Guadalcanal was ours. The shoestring operation, begun as a desperate attempt to check the pace of the Japanese advance, had ended in a major victory —our first on the ground—of the Pacific War. The tide had begun to turn.

4

Headed for Rabaul

In Papua, meanwhile, the Japanese on the Kokoda Trail had fought their way to The Gap, the pass at the highest point in the Owen-Stanley Mountains, and had pushed through it, down the southern slopes, toward Port Moresby. General Horii's forces outnumbered the Australians by at least two to one, and the Japanese were better equipped for the terrible mountain-and-jungle terrain. The Australians, for instance, were fighting with heavy .303 caliber rifles which were too awkward and slow on a jungle-mountain trail. By the middle of September, the Japanese had reached Ioribaiwa, only thirty miles from Port Moresby.

Then their orders changed. Colonel Edson's ma-

rines on Bloody Ridge, 700 miles away, had forced
the Japanese to alter their plans and postpone the
attack on Port Moresby. General Horii's men were
to hold as much of the Kokoda Trail as they could,
but the main Japanese objective was simply to defend
the Buna-Gona beachhead, marking time. The Port
Moresby attack would have to wait until the Guadalcanal attack had succeeded—as, of course, it never
did.

The Australians at Ioribaiwa promptly felt the ef-
fects of the new Japanese decision. Horii's men no
longer fought like demons every time they were
challenged. On the contrary, they gave ground easily.
The Australians, somewhat surprised, began pushing
them back along the Kokoda Trail toward Buna.
When this good news reached MacArthur's Australian
headquarters, preparations for an Allied attack on
Buna-Gona were hurried along. The 7th Australian
Division and the United States 32nd Infantry Division would make the assault. The big question was
how to move troops and supplies to the battlefield.
Even if the Allies could retake the Kokoda Trail—
which remained to be seen—a second route was required.

One battalion of the 32nd Division reconnoitered
a parallel trail farther east, a zigzag path across the
mountains so difficult that no white man had tried

to use it for a quarter of a century. The march was a back-breaking ordeal. Most of the battalion survived it, but their struggles proved that some other solution had to be found.

The answer: an air lift.

We discovered several places where airstrips could be built, or existing jungle landing fields could be improved. While the Australians fought their way back along the Kokoda Trail, two of the 32nd Division's regiments flew over the mountains, landed on the improvised strips, and then marched the rest of the way to the Buna-Gona front.

By November 16th, the Allied troops, organized into combat teams, were set to attack. As soon as they moved forward against the Japanese beachhead, they ran into serious trouble. The enemy's troops were concentrated in a fairly small area. They were skillfully dug in, and their positions were well camouflaged. Japanese snipers seemed to be everywhere.

The Allied soldiers were quickly halted. Japanese rifle, mortar, and machine-gun fire pinned them down. The American troops were getting their first taste of combat; they were baffled by skillful Japanese tactics.

At the end of two weeks, the 32nd Division had suffered 500 casualties without making any real headway. The Japanese opposition was very tough. The rain was coming down hard. Our men were falling out with malaria, dengue fever, and dysentery. Supplies were not getting through properly, and the American forces had almost no heavy weapons—flame throwers, tanks, or artillery—capable of blasting the Japanese out of their well-built bunkers. On the left of the Allied line, heading for the town of Gona, the Australians (reinforced by one battalion of the 32nd) were doing slightly—but only slightly—better.

MacArthur was furious. He sent General Robert L. Eichelberger to the front to take over the command and speed things up.

By the end of the first week in December, the situation was improving. The flow of supplies increased. Slowly, one strongpoint at a time, we began to penetrate the Japanese lines.

A tiny American force—one platoon commanded by Staff Sergeant Herman Bottcher—forced itself all the way through the enemy's defenses just east of Buna and reached the beach. There it dug in. Bottcher had eighteen riflemen and one machine gun, which he himself fired.

The Japanese were outraged. It was ridiculous for Bottcher's platoon to be there, far ahead of the rest of the Americans. But Bottcher saw nothing strange about it—and furthermore, he intended to stay. Every time the Japanese attacked, Bottcher's platoon was

ready for them. The beach at "Bottcher's Corner"—
as it was promptly christened—began to pile up with
Japanese dead who couldn't be buried for the time
being. Before too long, other American units followed
in Bottcher's footsteps.

On December 9, 1942, there was more good news.
The Australians, on our extreme left, had smashed
their way into Gona. The Japanese had been making,
and continued to make, desperate attempts to reinforce their Buna-Gona defense. The Allied air force,
patrolling the seas with B-17 and B-25 bombers, made
that job difficult. Reinforcements set sail repeatedly,
only to be caught, bombed, and driven back. Near
the end of December, sailing under cover of darkness,
the Japanese finally managed to land 800 reinforcements near Giruwa, at about the middle of the beachhead.

But the fresh Japanese troops were too late, and too
few, to slow the accelerating pace of the Allied advance. Eight United States tanks arrived just before
Christmas—as nice a present as the Allied troops had
ever had. They were General Stuart M3's, and from
the moment they went into action our infantry attacks
picked up speed. By January 3, 1943, Buna had fallen.
By January 22nd, the entire beachhead was in Allied
hands.

The victory had been won at a terrible cost: Australian and American casualties, combined, came to 8,500 killed and wounded—not counting those men who were laid low by sickness. The Japanese casualties were at least twice that bad.

The great point was, however, that Port Moresby was finally out of danger. In fact, it began to be obvious, as the year 1943 began, that the Japanese might have a hard time protecting Rabaul, their main base for operations in the entire South Pacific area.

Or so we hoped. If you look at the map, you will see that the eastern coast of New Guinea and the chain of Solomon Islands both point to New Britain. The Allied commanders were not sure which was the better route to Rabaul. MacArthur favored the New Guinea way, but it required a good many additional soldiers; and the fighting in North Africa, where we were now moving in toward Tunis, was using all our trained troops. Admiral Ernest J. King, commander in chief of the United States Fleet, thought we would do better to climb up the ladder of the islands to Bougainville starting from Guadalcanal.

The compromise was to follow both paths, keeping the Japanese as confused as possible about where the next blow would land.

Buna had barely been secured before Halsey's marines, operating from Guadalcanal, moved into the Russell Islands—the next small step up the ladder.

The landings went so smoothly and quickly that it was days before the Japanese even knew they had lost another piece of their stolen property.

One week later—on March 1, 1943—the crew of one of our Liberators on patrol, struggling back to Port Moresby through a violent tropical storm, spotted a vast Japanese convoy off the coast of New Britain. Its six troop transports and two freighters, with eight destroyers for an escort, stretched out over twenty miles of water. The Japanese were attempting to move their 51st Division from Rabaul, through the Bismarck Sea, down the Vitiaz Strait to Huon Gulf, where they planned to make their next major stand against the Allied ground forces.

Word was immediately flashed to Port Moresby and, starting the next day, swarms of Allied planes shuttled over the Owen-Stanley Mountains, pouring destruction down on the Japanese ships. At one time there were 109 assorted Allied planes participating in the attack. By nightfall, four of the eight Japanese destroyers and all but one of the ships in the convoy were sunk. Before dawn PT boats went out and disposed of that lone survivor.

That Battle of the Bismarck Sea, as it was called, cost the Japanese half of their 51st Infantry Division. It also demonstrated to the Japanese the danger of trying to supply Huon Gulf by convoy from Rabaul.

Still, they had been in possession of Lae and Salamaua for more than a year, which had given them time to prepare their positions. This was their last good place to try to stop the Allied advance up the New Guinea coast.

MacArthur's small amphibious force made a landing just south of Salamaua on the last day in June and began to push against the southern end of the Japanese-controlled sector. That same day, on the other side of the Solomon Sea, Admiral Halsey's men hit hard against the Japanese on Rendova Island. Five days later they attacked New Georgia, storming the big Japanese bases at Munda, where the Japanese, with a 5,000-man force, were prepared to put up a tremendous battle.

So much was going on in so many places that the Japanese scarcely knew which way to turn. Halsey made brilliant use of his amphibious forces, organized out of six Army and Marine divisions. Airfields on the islands were what interested him most. Each one gave him land-based air support for his next attack. Whenever Japanese troops could be isolated and contained, Halsey was perfectly happy to leave them where they were, hopelessly cut off, and hurry on to his next objective.

It was nearly two months, for example, before the last Japanese defenders on New Georgia were wiped out. But Halsey's men had been ashore only ten days before another outfit was set to deliver Halsey's next fast punch. The target was Kolombangara Island.

But the large Japanese garrison entrenched behind strong fortifications at Kolombangara proved exceedingly tough. Halsey by-passed it and headed for Vella Lavella, the next island to the north.

The Japanese had to rescue the Kolombangara garrison, if they could. They had been using barges to reinforce and supply the various detachments that Halsey's island-hopping advance had left behind. The flat bottoms and shallow draft of the barges allowed them to hug the islands' coasts by night, keeping out of the way of our deepwater patrols, and to duck into coves or hide along shore lines during the day.

The versatile PT boats were the best answer we had. Lieutenant John F. Kennedy, the skipper of PT boat 109, was on patrol between Kolombangara and Vella Lavella, hunting for Japanese barges, when a Japanese destroyer, looming up out of the night, rammed his ship and cut it in two. By a series of near miracles, Kennedy and the ten survivors of his twelve-man crew managed to swim to a small nearby island; and, after days of gallant efforts to attract attention, they were rescued.

Halsey's island-hopping technique kept the Japanese completely off balance and demanded heroic

(Left) A marine fighter plane takes off from the captured Munda Point airfield. (Below) American troops storm the beaches of Rendova Island.

efforts on the part of Halsey's fleet. Before the landing on Vella Lavella could be made, Vella Gulf had to be cleared. Six United States destroyers went in to battle a larger Japanese task force. The action was short. In the first minute, our ships fired twenty-four torpedoes with deadly aim. Two of the Japanese ships shuddered with the explosions, and a third blazed into towering flames.

As soon as the way was open, and air cover from Munda Field on New Georgia was available, Halsey put 4,600 men ashore.

By September 27th, we were operating the airfield at Barakoma on Vella Lavella. The strong Japanese force on Kolombangara, which had been by-passed, was now caught in a vise. It could be attacked by air from Munda, to the south, and Barakoma, to the north.

On the night of September 28th, the Japanese navy, using close to one hundred barges, tried to take the troops off Kolombangara. But our destroyer striking forces were ready and waiting, and in the course of that night, and during the four nights that followed, they sank one third of the barges in the Japanese rescue flotilla.

A week later the Japanese were also ready to concede Vella Lavella to Halsey's men.

That left only one more Japanese island on Halsey's

list: Bougainville—the northernmost, and largest, of the Solomons.

While Halsey's and MacArthur's men were broiling under the tropical sun, other American forces were fighting under arctic conditions in the Aleutians. In January, 1943, we had partly countered the Japanese seizure of Attu and Kiska by occupying Adak and Amchitka, building airfields, and keeping the Japanese garrisons under almost daily aerial bombardment. In May, a powerful task force took the Japanese at Attu by surprise. Fighting in snow drifts as much as ten feet deep, the Americans blasted the enemy out of its trenches and bunkers. Then we used the airfield on Attu, which the Japanese had started to build, to launch air strikes against Kiska.

It was August 15th before a task force of Americans and Canadians was ready to make the amphibious assault on Kiska. This time the Allies were surprised. The Japanese, foreseeing that Attu's seizure spelled Kiska's downfall, had stealthily evacuated the island by submarine under the thick white cover of a handy fog bank. When Allied troops rushed ashore, they found, to their delight, that Kiska was deserted.

The Aleutians were back in our hands.

Meanwhile, MacArthur's forces in the Salamaua-Lae sector were winning a spectacular victory. Instead of attacking Salamaua head on, MacArthur by-passed it. He landed the 9th Australian Division near Lae, north of Salamaua. And behind Lae, at the same time, American paratroopers dropped into the fields of tall reeds, where they quickly carved out an area large enough to contain a usable airstrip.

Before they finally realized what was happening, the Japanese in the Huon Gulf area were encircled. Salamaua fell first, on September 11, 1943. Five days later, Lae was in the Allies' hands. Then MacArthur, taking full advantage of this stunning victory, quickly pushed forward to Finschhafen and beyond, seizing control of the entire Huon Peninsula.

These bold successes were possible because, as an accompaniment to the attack, General George Kenney's fliers had smashed the Japanese air base at Wewak, on New Guinea's northern coast. Close to three hundred Japanese planes had been damaged or destroyed in a series of raids that robbed the Japanese of the air power they needed to defend northwest New Guinea. This meant, among other things, that Allied warships could sail into the Vitiaz Strait, between New Guinea and New Britain, without much danger of a Japanese attack from the air.

Halsey's troops had landed in the Treasury Islands. Halsey pretended (by landing the 2nd Marine Parachute Battalion) that Choiseul was to be his objective.

The feint worked. On November 1st, Halsey invaded Bougainville, catching the Japanese partly off guard.

Empress Augusta Bay, halfway up the island's west coast, was the landing place. The Japanese navy did its best to disrupt the assault, but plenty of sea and air support was on hand to help General Vandegrift's marines, including the carriers *Saratoga* and *Princeton*. A hard naval battle decided the issue. When it was over, the Japanese task force had been forced to retire. The landings proceeded on schedule.

There were months of hard fighting on Bougainville. It was March, 1944, before we could count the whole island as secure. But Halsey, none the less, had reached the top of the Solomons ladder.

While the Japanese were struggling with the problem of preventing an advance inland from Empress Augusta Bay, MacArthur's forces delivered another blow. On December 26, 1943, the 1st Marine Division landed on New Britain, at Cape Gloucester. American forces were only 275 miles from Rabaul.

The New Britain terrain, the marines soon discovered, was at least as bad as Guadalcanal; and the Japanese, desperately anxious to protect Rabaul from the ever-approaching Allied forces, fought like demons.

One sign of desperation was their moving 173 of their main fleet's carrier airplanes from Truk Island

After twenty-three days in Cape Gloucester's front lines, these weary marines are headed for a rest camp.

Marines on Bougainville fight desperately to hold their line.

to Rabaul. The Japanese used them to attack our beachhead at Empress Augusta Bay, and our convoys in the Solomon Sea, night and day. They sacrificed 120 carrier aircraft in this effort, plus seventy other planes, and all they managed to achieve was the sinking of one of our warships, and serious damage to three others.

It didn't take Halsey's Bougainville force long to get an air base operating. The distance by air to Rabaul was less than 300 miles. Fighter planes, as well as bombers, were in position to strike at the Japanese base.

As 1943 came to a close, Rabaul's fate was sealed.

Before ordering a final ground assault on Rabaul, the Joint Chiefs of Staff in Washington agreed that we could do better than spend quantities of men and materials on a siege that might take months. Rabaul could be encircled, cut off, and devastated by bombing —in very much the way Halsey and MacArthur had been skipping past Japanese strongpoints in the Solomons and in New Guinea.

During the first five months of 1944, the Allies accomplished that encirclement. In February, New Zealand troops captured an air base on Green Island, only 120 miles to the east of Rabaul. The United States Army landed in the Admiralty Islands in the north Bismarck Sea. At the same time, the troops on

New Britain slogged forward from Cape Gloucester through the steaming jungle, until almost the entire western third of the island was under Allied control.

There were close to 100,000 Japanese in the Rabaul garrison. But now that tremendous force was neutralized. Like the base itself, they were as useless as if they had all been taken prisoner.

5

The Marauders in Burma

The Allies had also decided to try to clear the Japanese out of northern Burma in an effort to reëstablish land communications with China. China had been isolated since the spring of 1942, when the Japanese had overrun Burma, cutting the Burma Road supply route, and putting a temporary stop to the delivery of United States aid to Chiang Kai-shek's armies.

Before that, the United States had been sending war supplies to China through Rangoon, Burma. They had gone by railroad to Lashio, Burma, and from there, by truck, over the Burma Road to Kunming and Chungking in China.

The Allies knew that, in order to keep China in

the war, they had to deliver quantities of all kinds of military supplies to her. In an attempt to make up for the loss of the Burma Road, the United States had organized a fantastic air transport system to fly the most essential supplies into China from the Assam region of India. Our pilots had been crossing "The Hump"—500 miles of wilderness in the Himalayas, the highest mountains in the world—with heavily laden transport planes. But air transport had been able to deliver only 6,000 tons of arms, ammunition, and fuel a month. That wasn't nearly enough.

The Allies hoped, in time, to reopen the Burma Road. But, first, if it could be managed, they wanted to recapture the tiny town of Myitkyina in northern Burma. That would immediately make the job of flying The Hump somewhat easier, because Japanese fighter planes based on the Myitkyina airstrip had been attacking the cargo planes every chance they had. With Myitkyina in Allied hands, the air transport pilots could fly a more southerly course over slightly less terrifying mountains and with less danger of Japanese interception.

There was one American combat force in China— the United States Fourteenth Air Force, commanded by Major General Claire Chennault. It was operating from fields deep in China, doing a remarkable job with inadequate supplies. Chennault's men were hit-

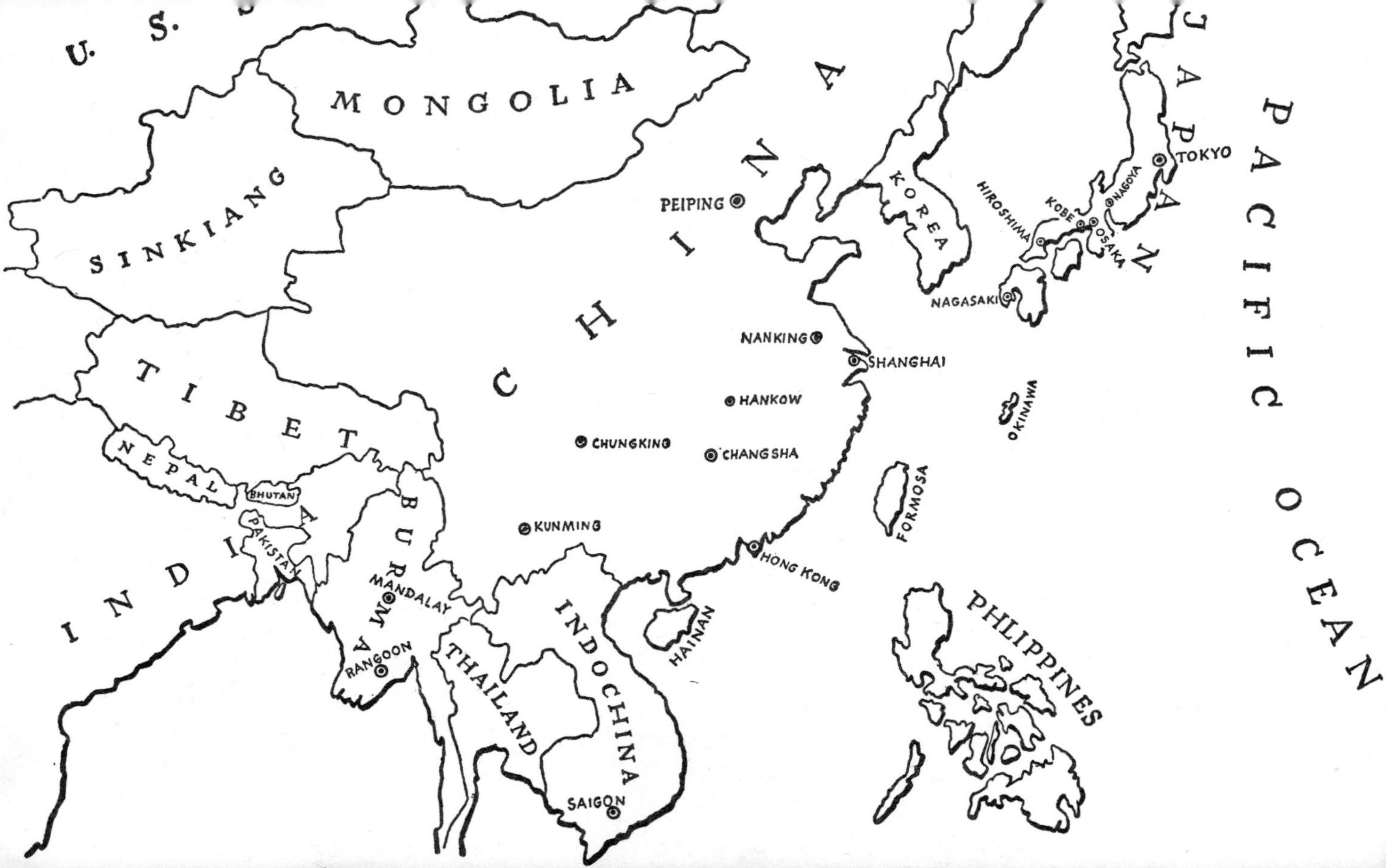
U.S.S.R.
MONGOLIA
SINKIANG
TIBET
NEPAL
BHUTAN
PAKISTAN
INDIA
BURMA
MANDALAY
RANGOON
THAILAND
INDOCHINA
SAIGON
HAINAN
CHINA
PEIPING
NANKING
SHANGHAI
HANKOW
CHUNGKING
CHANGSHA
KUNMING
HONG KONG
KOREA
JAPAN
TOKYO
NAGOYA
KOBE
OSAKA
HIROSHIMA
NAGASAKI
OKINAWA
FORMOSA
PHILIPPINES
PACIFIC OCEAN

ting Japanese targets from Indochina to southern Japan. The Allies hoped to supply the Fourteenth Air Force with more of everything, especially gasoline.

And an American officer, Major General Joseph "Vinegar Joe" Stilwell, had been serving with Chiang Kai-shek's armies for a long time as an observer and an active adviser. He was near Ledo, India, in 1943, reorganizing and training an army of Chinese troops who had been in Burma before the Japanese invasion, together with some Chinese soldiers who had been flown to Ledo from China.

American army engineers went to work turning what had been a mere mountain trail from Ledo into Burma into a fairly good road. They meant to extend it, finally, to Myitkyina and beyond.

Meanwhile the British, who had known little about jungle fighting when Hong Kong and Singapore were going down to defeat, had learned a great deal. One British general, Orde Wingate, had become a specialist in guerrilla warfare. He had led his small, specially trained units on raids deep into northern Burma, almost as far as Mandalay. He called his men "Chindits," and trained them to move through the jungles like natives, getting along on minimum supplies and making a maximum of trouble for the Japanese.

The United States decided to follow Wingate's example. Our Army formed a special unit of about 3,000 men organized and trained in a similar way. They were to fight with Stilwell. Their commander was Frank Merrill, and thus the outfit got its nickname, "Merrill's Marauders."

Stilwell opened the attack south toward Myitkyina in late 1943. In February, 1944, Merrill's Marauders joined him, marching in from India with their horses and mules over the new Ledo Road. Northern Burma is mountainous jungle, as wild as any country in the

The first convoy to China moves over the Ledo-Burma Road.

world. The native Burmese tribes, the Kachins, helped the Marauders by acting as guides and warning the Americans when they wandered toward the Japanese encampments scattered through the area. Some members of our Office of Strategic Services had already parachuted into the jungle, made friends with the Kachins, and taught some of them how to shoot American weapons.

Merrill's assignment was to drive deep into Japanese-held territory, behind the enemy's position, to assist Stilwell's Chinese army. Within five days, the Marauders had forced the Japanese to make their first major withdrawal in Burma in two years.

The Marauders included a number of Japanese-Americans who knew Japanese—to the enemy's confusion. They could listen in to the Japanese on captured military radios. On one occasion, a Marauder crept through the jungle and got so close to a group of Japanese officers that he could hear what they were saying and report back with advance knowledge of the Japanese plans.

At Walawbum, a Japanese-held town about halfway to Myitkyina, one battalion of Marauders beat off an attack by a whole Japanese regiment. Merrill's men were dug in along the riverbank, well concealed in the heavy jungle foliage, when the Japanese began to shell their position. The Marauders sat out several

hours of heavy artillery and mortar fire. Luckily, the Japanese didn't know exactly where they were. Most of the shells passed close over their heads. The Americans didn't move. Then the Japanese infantry attacked in screaming, shouting waves, expecting to terrify the few Americans who had survived the bombardment. The Marauders didn't make a sound. They held their fire until the Japanese were forty yards away. Then they let go with everything they had. For five hours the Japanese attacked again and again. Finally they gave up. Three hundred and fifty Japanese were dead. The Marauders' casualties were negligible and not a single man had been killed.

But the Marauders were beginning to find Burma itself more dangerous than the enemy. They had stopped following trails; the narrow jungle pathways invited Japanese ambush. As they headed for their next objective, a village named Shaduzup, they marched cross-country. The jungle was infested with blood-sucking leeches, ticks, mites, and mosquitoes. Some of them carried disease germs for which Americans had no immunity at all.

The Marauders had to cut their way through the jungle by hand, and they depended entirely upon what supplies could be parachuted to them. Friendly natives let them use their tame elephants for bulldozers to clear space for one air drop, but while playing with elephants was fun, the long march was an exhausting struggle.

By the time they had captured Shaduzup, the Marauders had lost almost one-third of their original number, mostly to diseases such as malaria, dysentery, and typhus. It was still another ninety miles over another mountain-jungle ridge to Myitkyina. March and April are Burma's rainy season. At times the rain came down so hard that holes had to be cut in the canvas litters on which wounded men were carried to let the water run out. When the Marauders got word that they were expected to push on and take the airstrip at Myitkyina they thought that everybody in Stilwell's headquarters must be crazy.

Two Chinese regiments joined Merrill's three battalions—now totaling less than 1,000 men—and the final push began. The last long march began on May 1st, and it was worse than anything the Marauders had previously been through. "One thing that helped keep you going," an officer wrote later, "was the thought that this was the worst there could be. It was so bad it was preposterous."

By May 16th, the Marauders' 1st Battalion had reached the Namkwi River, only four miles from the airstrip. A patrol reported that the Japanese force guarding the field didn't seem very large. The next day, with the Chinese 150th Regiment, the Marauders closed in. For the first time since the campaign began, the Marauders were out in open country. The change, combined with the low fevers most of them were running, made them almost dizzy. They ran into thirty Japanese blocking the road from dug-in positions at the base of a big tree, and skillfully moved round them. The 1st Battalion reached the airstrip without firing a shot. At the same time, the Chinese, approaching from the other end of the field, were having a fairly easy time. The Japanese, with mortars, defended their position east of the landing field. The Chinese, with fixed bayonets, charged into the enemy's trenches. By 10:30 A.M., Stilwell's headquarters got the radio message it had been waiting for: "In the ring." That meant the Marauders were on Myitkyina field.

The main Japanese force—approximately 700 men —was defending the town of Myitkyina, not the airstrip. The worst of the battle was yet to come.

Allied planes began using the airstrip on the afternoon of the first day. All sorts of things, including an anti-aircraft battery, began to arrive—everything except the food and ammunition which were badly needed. Then bad weather closed in on the field, and for a time nothing landed.

The Marauders, after their amazing 500-mile campaign, were exhausted. The Chinese, trying to push from the airstrip into Myitkyina itself, got as far as

Supplies for Merrill's Marauders were delivered by parachute from transport planes.

the railroad station; but in the process they took crippling casualties. Japanese reinforcements began to pour in.

By the end of May, 1944, all but 200 of the original 3,000 Marauders had been evacuated. But they never had let go their hold on the airstrip. And the Japanese, though they threatened, never could retake it.

The fighting in the Myitkyina sector went on for three months before Stilwell's troops finally captured the town. The main job of cleaning the Japanese out of northern Burma then fell to the British. Fresh Chinese troops attacked down the Burma Road and got as far as Wanting. An American force pushed south from Myitkyina, along the Irrawaddy River to Bhamo. British troops, driving south from Imphal, India, fought their way past Kalewa.

By the end of the summer, northern Burma was clear enough for the Allies to extend the Ledo Road past Myitkyina to Wanting, and construction of a fuel-oil pipeline from India to China was making rapid progress. By the end of the year, the Japanese all along their front were gradually withdrawing to the south.

A difficult mission had been accomplished.

6

Approaching the Philippines

When the Japanese base at Rabaul was sealed off, in the spring of 1944, a second phase in the war had come to an end.

Allied strategists, looking far ahead, tried to figure out how we could bombard and, if necessary, invade the Japanese islands. There was such a long way to go that planning for victory seemed rather premature, but in war everything depends on good strategy—and on realizing that all military plans are subject to change.

The Allies thought that they would eventually bomb Japan from air bases in eastern China. And, since the supply routes from India through Burma were so difficult, it looked as if the Allies would first have to land somewhere on the China coast, perhaps near Hong Kong. Before we could do that, we would need to win control of the South China Sea.

The further one speculated, the more complicated the matter got!

In order to control the South China Sea, the Allies would have to capture Formosa or recapture Luzon —very likely both. Certainly, in any case, our return to the Philippines—to one of the islands south of Luzon, which had now become a formidable Japanese stronghold—could not be accomplished a moment too soon. The immediate strategic question was how to get there.

The two possible routes offered a choice oddly like the old question of the best approach to Rabaul.

One way was through the Central Pacific, island-hopping from the Gilberts, to the Marshalls, to the Marianas, to the Carolines, to the Palaus—and so to the Philippines. It had a great attraction: the new American bombers, the B-29s ("Superfortress"), had enough range to reach Japan from the Marianas; we could begin to bomb the enemy's war plants as soon as we had taken those islands.

But the other way—across the north coast of New Guinea, and through the Moluccas Islands—was considerably shorter, since MacArthur's troops were al-

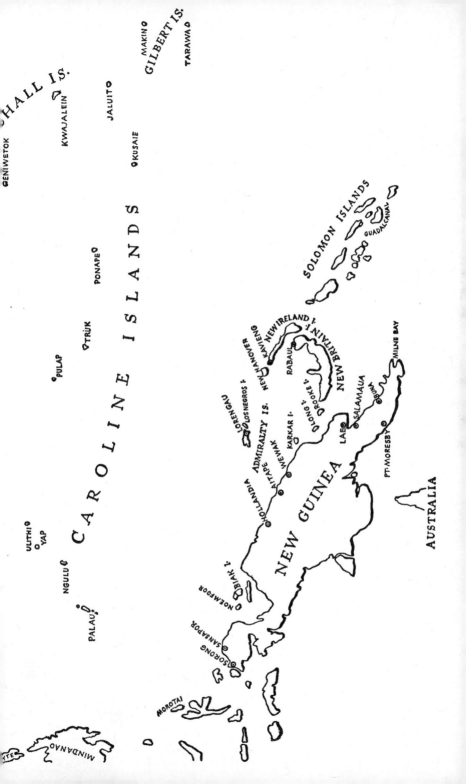

ready established in northeast New Guinea. The drawback was the length of the supply line from the United States to Australia and then north to the New Guinea front.

The American Joint Chiefs of Staff made a decision like the one they had made before: to follow both routes at once, keeping the Japanese defenses divided, off balance, and (they hoped) confused.

We had already won a position in the Gilberts, a scattering of coral atolls on the equator. In November, 1943, while the Japanese were busy trying to protect Rabaul, the marines had landed on Tarawa, in the Gilberts.

It was as violent and bloody a battle as any in the whole war. Most of the 2,600 first-rate Japanese soldiers were concentrated on Betio Island, at Tarawa's southwestern tip, guarding the airstrip. The tiny sliver of land bristled with coast defense guns, machine guns, anti-landing obstacles, and barbed wire. Admiral Shibasaki, the Japanese commander, thought he could stop any amphibious attack at the water's edge.

For a time it looked as if Shibasaki was right. The United States 2nd Marine Division, commanded by Major General Julian Smith, was met by a savage hail of gunfire. Many of his landing craft grounded on reefs far out from the beach. The marines were forced to wade in as far as 500 yards in a few places, and even

Amid wreckage and destruction two marines man a machine gun on Tarawa.

those who made it to the shore found little safe cover. Some companies lost half their men the first day.

The wonder was that, by the time it got dark, the marines had gained a toe hold some 300 yards deep and about 700 yards wide. It could hardly be called a beachhead—it was not much more than a cluster of fighting men, huddled in shell holes and foxholes, who were determined to hang on.

Late on the afternoon of the second day, Colonel David Shoup sent a message from Betio to division headquarters, on board the battleship *Maryland:* "We are winning."

It would have been an exaggeration to say so any earlier in the battle, but now the Japanese were being forced to give ground, a yard at a time. By the fourth day, Betio was secure. Once Betio had fallen, the rest of Tarawa was captured fairly easily.

We had practically wiped out the Japanese force, but our losses were staggeringly high: 837 marines were dead, and another 2,500 were wounded or missing in action.

There was one compensation for Tarawa's terrible human cost: the lessons learned there saved lives in every other amphibious landing for the rest of the war.

The Marshall Islands were our next target in the Central Pacific—a collection of about thirty-two atolls and 867 reefs scattered over 400,000 square miles of ocean. The Japanese took it for granted that we were coming. What astonished them was that, of all the choices he had, Admiral Nimitz decided to strike straight for Kwajalein, in the very center of the Marshalls. The 7th Infantry Division and the 4th Marine Division made the assaults, after Vice Admiral R. A. Spruance's Fifth Fleet (including Rear Admiral Marc Mitscher's Carrier Task Force 58) had delivered the combat troops to the beaches and had given them more fire support, for a longer time, than any of our amphibious attacks had ever had before. That was one of Tarawa's lessons.

During one phase of the preliminary bombardment, two shells per second—including 14-inch armorpiercing projectiles fired by the support battleships—landed on Kwajalein. When the big guns stopped booming, carrier-based aircraft bombèd and strafed and fired rockets. The ground behind the main landing beach was turned into rubble. As one observer commented, "The entire island looked as if it had been picked up to 20,000 feet and then dropped."

There were still a surprisingly large number of Japanese on Kwajalein alive and ready to fight, but they could do nothing in the face of the well-coördinated power of the invasion forces. An amphibious assault against a well-defended beach is considered the most difficult of all military operations, but Kwajalein went about as smoothly as any such attack can. The toughest Japanese opposition developed after our main strength was ashore. But by the end of a week—well ahead of schedule—the entire atoll was in American hands.

Kwajalein had gone so well, in fact, that our reserves—the 22nd Marines and the 106th Infantry—hadn't been used at all. This gave Nimitz a marvelous chance to strike almost immediately on his next target, 350 miles northwest of Kwajalein—Eniwetok Atoll. It was almost as if the Kwajalein operation had enough momentum left over to take a second objective.

In order to deceive the Japanese about our intentions—and, if possible, get in another stunning blow against the Japanese fleet—we planned a simultaneous carrier task force strike against Truk.

These operations were planned with incredible speed, and both forces were ready to attack by February 17th, less than two weeks after the completion of the Kwajalein mission.

Eniwetok, in the northwest corner of the Marshalls, is almost a perfect circle—a reef of small islands around a lagoon that is about twenty miles wide. More Japanese were stationed there than on Kwajalein, but fewer of them were combat troops. They had been ordered to defend the atoll to the death, but Eniwetok's defensive constructions—gun emplacements, pill boxes, and the like—couldn't compare with Kwajalein's or Tarawa's.

If you think of the whole circular atoll as resembling the face of a clock, it may help you to follow the invasion locations more easily. The invading force stormed ashore without too much trouble on Canna and Camellia—at the two o'clock position. Then they took Zinnia, at twelve o'clock. On D-plus-one they captured Engebi Island, at the one o'clock location. On D-plus-two, the marines landed on Eniwetok Island, toward the south end of Eniwetok Atoll—in roughly the five o'clock position. Here the Japanese opposition was strong. As soon as the 22nd Marines hit the sandy beach they came under mortar and machine-gun fire. Company B of the 1st Battalion ran into a Japanese strongpoint that had been left intact by the preliminary naval gunfire and air bombardment. It was a network of foxholes and connecting trenches in the shape of a spider's web.

As the marines moved inland, the Japanese fired from one position, and then quickly moved to another spot in the web. Second Lieutenant Ralph W. Hills and Private First Class William Hollowiak found themselves caught in the middle of this tricky installation. For a time both men hugged the ground, waiting for Japanese soldiers to appear. It was too slow a method, and meanwhile the Japanese infantrymen were picking off too many of the platoon's members. While Hills covered him, Hollowiak crawled forward, fired into one of the foxholes, lifted the palm fronds off the connecting trench, and threw in a hand grenade. Then Hollowiak covered Hills while the platoon commander repeated the process on the next position in the web. The two marines scrambled forward, gathering ammunition from the dead Japanese along the way, until they had demolished seven or eight positions in quick succession. All by themselves they had killed some twenty of the enemy's soldiers. Company B's advance, which had been delayed, could proceed.

By February 23, 1944, all of Eniwetok Atoll was under American control—and so, by that token, were the Marshalls as a whole, although countless undefended or lightly defended atolls still had to be occupied. By striking boldly at the key positions, Admiral Nimitz had ruined whatever chance the Japanese might have had to defend the group of islands.

Meanwhile, at Truk, Task Force 58 had made a fascinating discovery. Mitscher's mighty flotilla (five carriers, four light carriers, six battleships, ten cruisers, and twenty-eight destroyers) had arrived off Truk on the seventeenth of February—just when the ground troops were heading in for Eniwetok. The first fighter sweep of seventy planes had attacked the Truk airfields at dawn, destroying a grand total of 250 enemy planes, both on the ground and in the air.

But the surprise was that Admiral Mineichi Koga, realizing that time was running out for Truk, had withdrawn almost all of the main Japanese fleet. (He was headed, it was later discovered, for a new base at Palau.) The task force had to be content with wrecking the airstrips and sinking about 200,000 tons of merchant shipping still in the harbor—plus two light cruisers and three destroyers, the tail end of the fast-

A dive bomber gets the take-off signal before heading to blast one of the Japanese bases in the Central Pacific.

disappearing Japanese fleet.

Nimitz had assumed, until now, that we would eventually have to land troops on Truk. If, on the contrary, we could by-pass the Japanese stronghold as we had by-passed Rabaul, he could proceed fairly quickly with the invasion of the Marianas.

The next great blow against Japan's defenses was in New Guinea. On April 22nd—a month or two ahead of schedule—MacArthur's forces made an astonishing leap forward across the northern coast of the huge island. They by-passed the entire Japanese 18th Army at Wewak and Hansa Bay to land at Hollandia. The Japanese were completely surprised. On paper the maneuver seemed impossible, because Hollandia was beyond the range of our land-based fighter planes. Consequently, the Japanese had barely started to prepare its defenses, though Hollandia was an obvious prize.

MacArthur's secret weapon was Mitscher's Task Force 58, fresh from its strike against Truk. Mitscher's carrier planes covered the Hollandia landings and in record time we had airstrips at Aitape and Hollandia in operation so that MacArthur's invasion forces could supply their own air support.

Just one month later, on May 17th, MacArthur sent the 41st Division to seize Wakde Island. It was a jump of 120 miles. Ten days later, after Wakde had been secured, the 41st (less one regimental combat team) hit the beaches of Biak Island, 180 miles farther west.

These moves were so fast and so bold that, in every case, the Japanese were less than half ready to meet MacArthur's brilliant thrusts. With each leap his forces were prodding painfully deep into what the Japanese strategists regarded as their main line of resistance. In every case, the Japanese fought hard. And in the rear areas, where tens of thousands of by-passed Japanese soldiers tried to stave off their final defeat, the fighting was practically continuous.

Biak was a special case. MacArthur had no way of knowing that the Japanese high command hoped to launch a major counteroffensive in the South Pacific

area before the end of 1944. Biak was essential to the
Japanese plan, for there were three good airports in
a cluster on Biak's southern shore—precisely the airports the Allies wanted for their continued push toward the Philippines.

The first of these, Mokmer Drome, was captured
in eleven days' time after fairly stiff Japanese resistance. But neither Mokmer nor the other two airports
could be repaired and put into use until the Allies
had also cleared the Japanese off the low ridge not far
to the north of our most advanced position.

A rugged battle developed.

The only place on the front as important as Biak,
in the Japanese estimation, was the Mariana Islands.
Since, at the end of the first week in June, the Allies
had not yet made a move toward that group of islands,
the Japanese took a daring step. The Biak defenses
were reinforced by fresh Japanese troops.

The fight for the Biak ridge might have continued
for a long time if, on June 15th, Japanese headquarters
hadn't heard the news they dreaded: the United States
Pacific Fleet was in the Marianas, lying off the island
of Saipan.

The Japanese fleet, forgetting Biak in the face of a
greater emergency, raced to defend Saipan. The Allied
grand strategy was working perfectly. The twin drives
toward the Philippines had the Japanese dashing con-

fusedly from one end of the vast theater to the other.

The amphibious force General Holland M. Smith was putting ashore on Saipan was the largest we had so far been able to assemble—three Marine divisions, two Army divisions, a Marine brigade, and special troops, a total of more than 77,000 men.

That in itself was a great achievement. Considering all the other men fighting on New Guinea, and the tremendous Anglo-American-Canadian invasion force in Europe, which had landed on the Normandy beaches only nine days earlier, the combat power of the United States seemed almost incredible.

But the Saipan invasion troops had no time to think about any such thing. Japanese artillery fire, which was heavy and accurate, demanded all their attention. Smith's attack had surprised the Japanese, but they had recovered quickly, and they fought furiously for every foot of ground.

By the fourth day, most of southern Saipan was under control. We had paid a terrible price of 5,000 casualties for it. In some units, sixty per cent of the men had been killed or wounded. The casualty lists included six battalion commanders.

On that same day—June 19th—as Smith's men reorganized in preparation for the drive into northern Saipan, the Battle of the Philippine Sea began. The

Troops and supplies in various types of landing crafts (above) move shoreward for the invasion of Saipan, while (below) the first wave of marines to hit the beach take cover behind a sand dune.

Japanese First Mobile Fleet was out to destroy Spruance's Fifth Fleet, and the Japanese were strong: three heavy carriers, six light carriers, and five battleships, commanded by Admiral Jisaburo Ozawa. The Japanese fleet could count, furthermore, on land-based air reinforcement from the many airstrips on the Japanese-held islands in the area.

But Spruance's navy was even stronger. He had seven heavy carriers, eight light carriers, and seven battleships—outnumbering the Japanese in every category. The temptation to sail west and meet the oncoming Japanese force was great. But Spruance's job was to protect the Saipan landing, and he stuck to his mission. He kept his ships fairly close to Saipan and Guam.

Admiral Ozawa, as he approached, launched his planes at their extreme range—350 miles—thinking that they could land on Guam, refuel and rearm, and hit the Americans a second time as they flew back toward their mother ships.

Ozawa was making a fatal error. Our land forces had been able to swarm all over the airfields on Guam, and the Japanese had no safe place to land.

As soon as Ozawa's planes took off, one of our patrolling submarines, the *Albacore,* shot the Japanese admiral's flagship, the *Taiho,* right from under him with a beautiful spread of six torpedoes. An hour later, the submarine *Cavalla* sent a second Japanese carrier to the bottom of the ocean.

That was only the beginning of a bad day for Ozawa (who had transferred safely to a third carrier). In a fantastic series of battles, our fliers, helped by our anti-aircraft gunners, destroyed 243 of the Japanese carrier planes. Another fifty land-based Japanese planes were shot out of the sky or bombed on the ground. By the time it got dark, Ozawa was beaten. Not more than 130 of his planes were left.

Task Force 58 set out immediately in pursuit. It steamed through the night, and late the following day, Mitscher's pilots took off from the carriers' decks. Only two hours of daylight were left. When they caught up with Ozawa it was 6:40 P.M. The likelihood of the fliers' getting back to their carriers in the dark, and at the extreme range, was already slim. But their chances were getting worse with every passing minute.

Nevertheless, Mitscher's brave men were determined to finish their job. They dived on the Japanese fleet and, in half an hour, they made a great score: one carrier sunk, and a battleship, a cruiser, and a light carrier seriously damaged.

Then they headed back. It was getting very dark,

and, although Mitscher knew that Japanese submarines were around, he permitted the lights to be turned on. Three-quarters of the planes found carriers—a fine record, considering the difficulties. As the others ran out of gas they splashed into the ocean. Our destroyers scurried around, looking for flashlight signals of distress. Two-thirds of the men who crash-landed were picked up; again, that was better than one might have expected. But when the final tally was made, forty-nine of our heroic fliers were not there to answer the roll calls. The bad odds, which they had faced with deliberate disregard, had caught up with them.

On July 10th northern Saipan fell to our ground attack, just about the same moment that the last Japanese organized defenses on Biak were collapsing. On both islands, though, isolated Japanese soldiers and small pockets of resistance continued to hold out for months to come. Among the Japanese dead on Saipan was Admiral Nagumo, who had commanded the carrier strike against Pearl Harbor.

These crippling defeats rocked the Japanese government. Tojo was relieved as the active head of the Japanese army and replaced by General Yoshijiro Umezu. Then on July 19th Tojo and his entire cabinet resigned from office. General Kujiaki Koiso succeeded him as premier.

The Allies were winning everywhere, just as the

Japanese had piled one success on another in the dark days of late 1941 and early 1942.

On August 9th, after twenty days of furious battle, the Marines completed the occupation of Guam. Once again, after two and a half years, the American flag flew over the island. Tinian, the island immediately south of Saipan, was taken at practically the same time.

In the South Pacific, MacArthur's forces were leaping ahead from Biak to Noemfoor (July 2nd); and from Noemfoor to Sansapor (July 30th) on the western tip of New Guinea. Sansapor is only 600 miles from Mindanao.

Kenney's bombers began to pound Mindanao— and all the Japanese installations between New Guinea and the Philippines—with thousands of tons of high explosive. They paid special attention to Morotai, the northernmost of the Moluccas Islands, which is just about halfway from Sansapor to Davao, in Mindanao.

On September 15th, MacArthur's amphibious forces —the 31st Infantry Division—invaded Morotai. On the same day, Halsey's Third Fleet covered landings on Peleliu and Angaur in the Palau Islands. The 1st Marine Division made the assault on Peleliu. There was not too much difficulty getting ashore, but the fighting that followed—lasting for two weeks—was as savage as any the veteran outfit had ever encountered.

Paratroopers drop onto Karmiri airstrip to reinforce the invasion troops already on Noemfoor Island.

Part of the 81st Infantry Division, which had secured Angaur without much difficulty, reinforced the marines. Our forces killed close to 11,000 Japanese on Peleliu alone before we could count the island as secure, and our own losses were tragically high. Before Japanese resistance in the Palaus ended, our dead numbered almost 2,000 and our total casualties— more than half of them marines—were five times that many.

Now the United States forces were poised for the move into the Philippines themselves. Since April they had advanced 1,870 miles from the Marshall Islands to the Palaus, and 1500 miles from Huon Gulf to Morotai. The two-pronged approach strategy, depending on the most skillful coördination of land, sea, and air forces, had proved a brilliant success.

7

The Philippines Recaptured

Where in the Philippines should the invading forces land?

MacArthur had planned to take Mindanao first and then move north to Leyte, but he was beginning to wonder whether the attack couldn't be speeded. Halsey thought that Leyte, well up toward the center of the group of islands, would be the better place to strike. Nimitz agreed.

Leyte it was. MacArthur set the invasion date for October 20, 1944.

The Central Philippine Attack Force, commanded by MacArthur, included the Seventh Fleet (Vice Admiral Thomas C. Kinkaid), the Sixth Army (Lieutenant General Walter Kreuger), and Kenney's Allied Air Force. Admiral Halsey's Third Fleet, which stayed under Nimitz's control, was to guard the northern flank of the invasion forces and do battle with the Japanese combined fleet, if and when it came out to fight.

Halsey took the Third Fleet on a daring series of raids against Formosa, Okinawa, and Luzon with the idea of crippling as much land-based Japanese air power as he could. The Third Fleet, by now, was gigantic. In cruising formation it covered an area forty miles long and nine miles wide. It did a wonderful job. In a few weeks the Fleet had destroyed 650 Japanese airplanes. In spite of this the Japanese talked themselves into believing that their airmen had smashed the Third Fleet. The Japanese newspapers announced a victory; the Japanese radio boasted of it for days. Since Halsey was operating under radio silence, the Americans were almost ready to believe the Japanese propaganda. Then Nimitz received Halsey's reassuring message: "All Third Fleet ships reported by Tokyo radio as sunk have now been salvaged and are retiring in the direction of the enemy."

Kreuger landed four divisions on the island of Leyte at ten o'clock in the morning of the 20th. The Japanese seemed surprised, and their resistance—except here and there—was feeble. By the end of the first

General Douglas MacArthur and a group of U.S. Army and Philippine officers wade ashore on their return to Leyte Island.

day, we had won two firm beachheads about seventy miles apart. One was just south of Tacloban, the capital of Leyte (where MacArthur, forty-one years earlier, had served right after his graduation from West Point). The other one was at Dulag.

Three days later, there was a small ceremony in front of the Tacloban City Hall.

"I have returned," MacArthur said. "By the grace of Almighty God our forces stand again on Philippine soil—soil consecrated in the blood of our two peo-

ples." Beside MacArthur was Sergio Osmeña, Quezon's
successor as president of the Philippines. He, with the
members of his cabinet, had returned with the invasion forces. The Philippine government was reëstab-
lished on Philippine soil.

So far, everything had gone remarkably well—sus-
piciously well, in fact.

The truth was that General Yamashita, the Japanese commander in the Philippines, had been told to
make a fight for Leyte. He had given orders that were
moving 45,000 Japanese soldiers toward Ormoc, on
the other side of the island.

It also seemed strange that the Japanese navy hadn't
yet made its appearance. Just after midnight on October 23rd, the United States submarine *Darter*, on
patrol with the *Dace* off Palawan Island, picked up
Japanese ships on her radar. The two subs attacked
at dawn. In the pink half-light, the *Darter* saw a
column of Japanese battleships flanked by cruisers.
She fired on the leading cruiser. Through his periscope the *Darter*'s captain saw (as he said later) that
"she [the cruiser] was belching flame from . . . the
forward turret to the stern."

When the *Dace* came up to periscope level, her
captain, seeing what the *Darter* had done, cried: "It
looks like the Fourth of July out there!" Then the
Dace fired on, and sank, a second Japanese cruiser.

The *Darter*'s victim, we later found out, was Admiral Takeo Kurita's flagship. Kurita transferred to his huge battleship, the *Yamato*, and steamed into the island-dotted waters of the Sibuyan Sea. He was taking his force toward the San Bernardino Strait, north of Samar Island, on his way to Leyte Gulf.

But now Halsey's planes were alerted by the *Darter* and the *Dace*. Third Fleet pilots spent the whole day attacking Kurita's fleet. They sank one battleship and damaged several others. Kurita reversed his course and began to sail west, the direction from which he had come.

Meanwhile, a second Japanese naval force had been spotted. It was sailing into the Mindanao Sea, apparently headed for Leyte Gulf by way of narrow Surigao Strait. Kinkaid ordered his Seventh Fleet to prepare for a night engagement, and he stationed his six battleships in a classic, textbook battle line at the north end of Surigao Strait. His cruisers were in front of the battleships. His destroyers guarded the line's right and left flanks, and his torpedo boats were strung out all the way down the Strait. Kinkaid's greatest worry was a shortage of armor-piercing shells. (His ships were loaded for shore bombardment, not for fighting another fleet.) It was decided that the battleships should hold their fire until the Japanese were less than 20,000 yards away.

PHILIPPINE SEA

SAMAR

⊙ CATBALOGAN

BILIRAN

DARAM

⊙ LIMON

TACLOBAN ⊙

L E Y T E

⊙ PALOMPON
ORMOC ⊙

⊙ DULAG

LEYTE
GULF

SULUAN

HOMONHON

CAMOTES IS·

CAMOTES SEA

SURIGAO STRAIT

DINAGAT

SIARGAO

PANAON

LEYTE CAMPAIGN
October—December 1944

MINDANAO

Admiral Nishimura, with two battleships, one heavy cruiser and four destroyers, was sailing into a perfectly laid trap. The engagement began at two o'clock in the morning. After Kinkaid's torpedo boats attacked, his destroyers, maneuvering brilliantly, broke up the Japanese formation. By the time the enemy column reached the Seventh Fleet's battle line, Nishimura had only one battleship, his cruiser, and one destroyer left. Five of Kinkaid's six battleships had been hit at Pearl Harbor. Now they got their revenge. At 4:19 A.M., Nishimura's flagship, the *Yamashiro*, capsized and sank. The Admiral and nearly all the members of his crew went down with her.

The Seventh Fleet had no time, however, to rejoice over its splendid defense of the southern approach to Leyte Gulf. At 6:45 A.M. word came that Kurita had reversed his course again, had passed through the San Bernardino Strait, and was steaming down the coast of Samar, approaching Leyte Gulf from the north.

Kinkaid had thought that Admiral Halsey's Third Fleet was guarding the San Bernardino approach.

It wasn't. Halsey's pilots had given him the impression that Kurita's force had been completely beaten in the Sibuyan Sea. And so Halsey, having spotted still a third Japanese task force, including two battleships and four aircraft carriers, well to the north of Leyte, had gone off to attack it.

Kurita was far from beaten. Despite his losses, he still had twenty-two warships. Five of them were battleships, led by the *Yamato,* the world's biggest.

For the time being, all that stood between Kurita's oncoming force and the American fleet of thin-skinned transports and supply ships in Leyte Gulf were three small baby-flattop task forces, nicknamed Taffy One, Taffy Two and Taffy Three. Each of these had at least four of the small carriers, escorted by a handful of destroyers and destroyer escorts. The baby flattops were painfully slow. They could do eighteen knots, only a little faster than half the speed of Kurita's dreadnoughts.

As the Japanese ships came steaming over the horizon, they ran straight into Taffy Three, commanded by Admiral Clifton Sprague. The *Yamato* opened fire with her 18-inch guns at a range of eighteen miles. There was just one thing for the small defending force to do: act as if it was a match for the Japanese—and hope to cause trouble enough to slow down Kurita's attack.

Our planes quickly took to the air. Our destroyers, destroyer escorts, and carriers all began making smoke to confuse the aim of the Japanese gunners. While our planes bombed and strafed, Admiral Sprague's three destroyers, in the face of overwhelmingly superior enemy fire power, headed straight for Kurita's great column of ships. The *Johnston's* gunners took on a heavy cruiser, the *Kumano;* and, before the *Johnston* was hit, her crew saw the burning *Kumano* forced to drop out of formation. The *Hoel* dashed into the midst of the Japanese fleet, her guns ablaze. She broke through the screen of cruisers and fought her way right up to the *Yamato*. The great battleship, forced to evade the *Hoel's* torpedoes, was driven out of position and, temporarily, out of the battle.

When the first attack was done, the American force attacked again. Our small carriers—unable to run away, and only lightly armored—seemed doomed. One of them, the *Gambier Bay,* had been hit several times, and was sinking. Still our destroyers, joined now by the destroyer escorts, were doing everything they could to distract the Japanese gunners. So were the planes from the carriers belonging to Taffy Two and Taffy One. The *Johnston,* though she had fired all her torpedoes, tried to break up a five-ship Japanese squadron (a cruiser and four destroyers) that was closing in on the crippled *Gambier Bay.* The *Johnston* made for the biggest ship, the cruiser, and scored twelve hits in quick succession. At the same time, the *Johnston* took a number of serious hits. The Japanese cruiser turned away and the *Johnston* attacked one of the destroyers.

Our flattops were twisting and turning, changing course as often and as quickly as possible, to make themselves difficult targets. And the *Johnston* had caused so much confusion that, when Kurita's ships fired their torpedoes at our carriers, every shot missed.

The *Johnston,* on the other hand, was doomed. She kept all her guns firing, but the Japanese scored one hit after another. In half an hour, the *Johnston* went down.

The Battle of Samar had lasted two hours. Though the Taffys didn't seem to have a chance left, it was marvelous that they had kept the fight going so long.

At 9:25 A.M. a surprising new development took place. To his amazement, the lookout on the bridge of Sprague's ship, the *Fanshaw Bay,* saw that Kurita's ships were retreating to the north. "They're getting away!" the man cried.

This was a perfect illustration of the fighting spirit that our men had shown all through the unequal battle. By refusing to admit for a moment that it was outclassed, Taffy Three had broken, baffled, and routed the enemy. The Japanese gunners had managed to sink only one flattop, two destroyers, and a destroyer escort. Now Kurita was forced to retire and re-form his fleet.

He never got a chance to resume his attack. As soon as our planes could land and reload, our three task forces launched new air strikes against the Japanese.

By noon Kurita had lost five cruisers, with three others badly damaged. Taffy Two's planes—fifty-six of them, thirty-seven carrying torpedoes—were swooping down in the biggest air strike of the day. Kurita had had enough. He turned north and ran.

American naval victories in the fighting around Leyte (including Halsey's success off Cape Engaño in the north, where the Third Fleet had sunk four carriers, a light cruiser, and three destroyers) had destroyed the Japanese navy. We had sunk twenty-six of their warships, and although we had lost six ships in doing so, we didn't need ours as badly as the Japanese needed theirs.

The Japanese were no longer able to assign their navy a mission of any kind—although, to be sure, a number of ships were still afloat.

On the other hand, the Japanese army was still tremendously powerful. Yamashita had 250,000 soldiers on Luzon alone, not counting the 45,000 reinforcements who were steadily disembarking on the west coast of Leyte, prepared to defend the island against Kreuger's advancing troops.

After its fast start, our Sixth Army ran into heavy tropical storms which turned the roads into ribbons of mud. The engineers found it almost impossible to build air bases on the wet ground. Our infantry lacked air support, and we were unable to use our land-based

planes to bomb the Japanese convoys landing reinforcements at Ormoc. Nevertheless we had cleared
the Leyte Valley by November 2nd, and were getting
ready to fight across the island's central mountain
range into Ormoc Valley, which was becoming a Japanese stronghold.

It was tough going. The Japanese constantly counterattacked, fighting desperately to hold Limon at
the Valley's northern end. It took the 32nd Division a
month to capture Limon. Meanwhile, in another amphibious assault, the 77th Division had gone ashore
at Ipil, just south of the town of Ormoc. Three days
later—on the same day Limon was captured—the 77th
entered Ormoc.

By Christmas, the Japanese were forced to admit
that the land battle for Leyte was lost. The fighting
lasted well into January, and the Japanese losses—a
total of close to 70,000 casualties—were far more than
they could afford.

MacArthur was ready to attack Luzon. The first
step was the seizure of the southwest corner of Min-
doro Island. That gave us an air base just 150 miles
south of Manila. Kenney's bombers quickly went into
action against the dwindling Japanese air force on
Luzon. On January 9, 1945, Kreuger's Sixth Army
landed on Lingayen Gulf—almost a repetition of the
Japanese assault in December, 1941. By nightfall,

we had 68,000 men ashore in a well-established beach-head. Within a day or two our advance down the Central Plains toward Manila was moving forward.

Yamashita was attempting to defend Japan by defending Luzon, and he fought a stubborn delaying action. His strength was concentrated in the mountains, on Kreuger's east flank, where the Japanese might be able to hold out for months.

MacArthur was eager to get to Manila as fast as possible. The Japanese were just as determined to keep him out as long as they could.

Our 11th Airborne Division landed at Nasugbu, south of Manila Bay, and began to race toward Manila from the southwest. The 1st Cavalry Division, which had fought its way south to Plaridel, organized two armored "flying columns" and sent them dashing toward the outskirts of the city.

Apart from military objectives, we were in a great hurry because we wanted to free the prisoners the Japanese had been holding for three terrible years. Tens of thousands had died. Women and children had been treated as brutally as our soldiers, whom the Japanese insisted on calling "captives," not prisoners-of-war.

The rescues began on January 30th. One company of American Rangers, reinforced by 500 Filipino guerrilla fighters, raided deep into Japanese-held territory and released the prisoners in a small camp at Cabanatuan. Almost immediately after that, the 11th Airborne captured a prison camp at Los Baños and freed a number of civilians who had been locked up there.

But most of our own soldiers—the pitifully few who were still alive—were interned in Manila itself. One prison camp was near Santo Tomas University, on the north side of the city. On Saturday afternoon, February 3rd, nine Marine pilots flew low over the camp. One of the pilots wrote a note, tied it to his goggles, and dropped it into the camp.

"Roll out the barrel," the note said. "Santa Claus is coming Sunday or Monday."

The message was too pessimistic. A moment later the prisoners heard the roar of engines, and a shout: "Where's the front gate?" It was a tank, belonging to the 1st Cavalry's flying squadron. We freed 3,700 prisoners that day, many of them women and children. By the next day, MacArthur's men had fought on into the city as far as Bilibid prison. Another 1,024 prisoners—all of them Allied soldiers—were rescued.

For another whole month the Japanese defended Manila, just as they fought everywhere in Luzon, with desperate ferocity. We had to blast them out, house by house. It was a dreadful process. The street fighting wrecked the beautiful city and, unavoidably,

U.S. infantry forces, with a 105-mm. howitzer motor carriage M7, advance into the town of Maguillian in northern Luzon.

A group of American soldiers march to an evacuation hospital after their liberation from a Japanese prison camp.

a great many civilians got hurt. The last Japanese took refuge in Intramuros, a tiny seventeenth-century section of modern Manila, surrounded, in the style of that time, by an ancient, thick wall. There they held out until March 4th.

By then Yamashita's army had been split into three separate forces. The strongest group was in the rugged mountains of northeastern Luzon. We couldn't ignore them because we intended, at the time, to use Luzon as a great supply base and the staging area for our final attack upon the Japanese islands. The bitter fighting continued all through the spring and summer—and right up to the end of the war. Yamashita did not plan to attack. But his holding action did what he wanted it to do: it occupied the full attention of three American divisions.

Meantime there were other islands to capture. While the Luzon fighting was in progress, the Americans had started two new campaigns. One was on Iwo Jima. The other was on Okinawa. Both were to serve as key bases for the final assault.

8

The Capture of Iwo Jima

In Japanese, "Iwo Jima" means "sulphur island." As far as we were concerned, the little island meant "air base." It was less than 800 miles from the enemy's capital, about halfway between Tokyo and the heavy-bomber fields on Saipan.

We wanted Iwo as an emergency landing field for any Superfortresses that might be having trouble on the return flight to Saipan. Also, as a base for our new P-51 fighters, Iwo would allow us to provide our heavy bombers with escorts to their targets and back.

American planes had been bombing Japan at an increasing pace since late October, 1944, and the damage we had done already was only a token compared to what General Henry "Hap" Arnold intended the Air Force to do. The Japanese, who could see what was in store for them, had put 20,000 men on Iwo's seven-and-one-half square miles, under the command of General Tadamichi Kuribayashi. They were determined to make the low, volcanic island into a fortress. Except for Mount Suribachi, an extinct volcano about five hundred feet high at Iwo's southern tip, Iwo's natural defenses did not amount to much. But the Japanese, mixing volcanic ash with cement, transformed the land into a concrete honeycomb of interconnecting strongpoints. Artillery, mortars, and antitank guns were emplaced in bunkers, reinforced with steel, whose walls were four feet thick. Tunnels ran under the airstrips, linking positions as far as 800 yards apart. Whole hills were hollowed out and reconstructed from the inside. There were a good many natural caves, too, and these were improved and wired for electricity. Some of them were big enough to hold 400 soldiers.

We had never encountered anything quite like it. Tarawa's defenses had seemed rugged. By comparison with Iwo's, they were crude.

It was obvious that Iwo would need a tremendous softening up before three Marine divisions could hope to storm it. Two and a half months before D-Day, Army, Navy and Marine Corps planes began to give

With helmets and faces camouflaged, an American assault force boards landing crafts for transport to Iwo Jima.

the tiny island a working-over, dropping 500-pound bombs every day in the week. Iwo began to look like the surface of the moon. Then, for the last three days before the invasion, Task Force 52—a great fleet, including battleships that had taken part in the Normandy landings and eleven escort carriers—concentrated all its fire power on Iwo.

At two minutes after nine o'clock on the morning of February 19th, the marines began to jog across the dirty gray sand of the invasion beaches.

For the first hour, it looked as if the record-breaking size of the preliminary bombardment had done most of the job. Only a few Japanese appeared, and the enemy's shellfire was light. Our main difficulty was the volcanic sand. Our guns, tanks, DUKWs, and amphibious half-tracks got stuck. The marines themselves sank in up to their calves, and their jog slowed to a difficult walk.

Then the entire island seemed to break into gunfire, all of it aimed at the invading traffic jam of men and equipment. Harmless-looking mounds of earth turned out to be the tops of concrete pillboxes and block-houses. The ground was sown with thousands of land mines. When our tracked vehicles managed to lumber off the beaches, they were met by deadly 47-millimeter gunfire.

It was a foretaste of horrors to come. Thirty thousand marines struggled ashore that first day, but their beachhead was dangerously shallow. Our casualties had been appalling.

Since the top of Mount Suribachi was a perfect artillery observation point, and some of the deadliest Japanese fire was being directed from there, it was our first objective.

On D-plus-one, after a sleepless night, the 28th Marine Regiment jumped off for Suribachi. The distance to the base of the mountain was short, but the going was extremely hard. Japanese pillboxes were concealed under piles of brush. The marines couldn't find them until they opened fire. Then each one had to be put out of commission with flame throwers and dynamite. By the end of the day, the 28th Marine Regiment had advanced only 200 yards. Twenty-nine marines were dead and 133 had been wounded.

The next day—D-plus-two—the American command risked a forty-plane air strike on Suribachi, although that meant that some bombs fell within 100 yards of our own forward positions. By afternoon, one battalion of the regiment got as far as the base of the mountain and dug in.

The face of the mountain was steep. Our bombing and the naval shellfire had destroyed the trails up Suribachi. That meant a hand-over-hand climb for the marines, past dozens of caves filled with desperate Japanese.

During the night there were two strong Japanese attempts to infiltrate the 28th's position. Both attempts were repulsed and, at dawn, the marines counted eighty-eight Japanese dead. The attack continued.

On D-plus-three, as the marines slowly inched their way up, it rained. The sandy ash which had already caused so much trouble turned to sticky mud, jamming our automatic weapons.

The Americans never did find out exactly how many

Japanese soldiers were defending Suribachi, for the 28th Marine Regiment, with the help of engineers, literally blasted their way from cave to cave. Whenever possible, they set off dynamite charges that brought the entrance to the Japanese strongholds crashing down in a pile of rocky rubble, sealing up the soldiers inside in a permanent tomb.

Finally, on D-plus-four, a few marines who had been climbing the mountain's northern face reached the crater on the top. They found a length of pipe and raised a small American flag they had with them—a signal, visible all over the island, of where they were. But the flag seemed too small. A few marines scrambled back down to the beach, borrowed a great big flag, carried it up the mountain, and raised it. The photograph of this second flag-raising, taken by Joe Rosenthal of the Associated Press, was to become the most famous picture of the Second World War.

The flag-raising wasn't the end of the battle for Iwo. It took the 28th Marines another week before Suribachi was completely clear of Japanese. (Many of the dead Japanese wore explosive charges strapped to their bodies. They had been ready to blow themselves up—if they got the chance—for the sake of knocking out an American position.) And in the northern part of the island, the fierce combat was still in progress.

By February 28th, we had seized the central section of Iwo, including the island's two airfields. The distance to the northern tip of Iwo was less than two miles, and we were advancing toward it, maintaining a fairly well-connected front across the island, with our three Marine divisions abreast, the 5th on the left, the 3rd in the middle, and the 4th on the right.

As the fighting progressed, the sparse greenery was burned or blasted away. The shattered rocks were twisted into fantastic shapes—partly from the bombings, and partly from earthquakes that had occurred back in the time when Suribachi was a live volcano. The landscape was laced with rocky ridges and narrow chasms, and everywhere there were Japanese hidden in their bunkers and burrows. Sulphur vapors steamed through crevices; in some places the ground was too hot to stand on.

Our troops slowly pushed north across this weird, unearthly terrain. The flank divisions were helped by supporting naval gunfire. Our warships steamed along both coasts, dueling with the heavy Japanese guns and preparing the way for another short infantry advance. The 5th Marines, firing rocket launchers mounted on trucks, blasted the ground ahead of them. Armored bulldozers cut rough paths through the rocks for our tanks. Our tanks fired on pillboxes and caves at point-blank range. Then their infantry escorts, with

(Left) Soldiers on Iwo Jima faced the difficult job of stalking Japanese snipers hidden in caves and holes. (Below) Two marines throw a scorching inferno at the mighty Japanese defenses which blocked the way to Mount Surabachi.

the engineers, would try to finish up the job.

Our troops couldn't afford to by-pass a single Japanese strongpoint. Even when we thought we had cleared all the Japanese from a stretch of ground two or three hundred yards long, it would turn out that some had escaped from an undetected tunnel at our rear, and were manning a gun position that had somehow been missed.

Our rate of casualties was frightful. Since there was no safe place on Iwo, the Americans lost an unreasonable number of commanders. Our battalion command posts seemed to be a favorite Japanese target. One battalion lost both its commanding officer and its executive officer at practically the same moment. In every such case, it put a terrible strain of responsibility on all the other officers.

A unit that is short of leaders is not likely to fight well, but in one case the death of an officer—1st Lieutenant Jack Lummus of the 27th Regiment—served to inspire his whole company. On March 8th, Lummus, one of the best-liked platoon leaders in his whole outfit, was leading his men through an intricate network of Japanese pillboxes. Lummus had destroyed three of the strongpoints practically single-handed. He kept going, and he kept his platoon going, although he had been wounded.

Then a land mine was exploded close to where Lummus lay, and the blast killed him.

That afternoon, Lummus' company fought like demons. They moved farther and faster than any outfit had for days. They smashed through the Japanese defenses and took the high ground they had been assigned—the bluffs overlooking the sea on Iwo's northern coast.

By March 10th, the 4th Marines, working up along Iwo's east coast, had come through the "Meat Grinder," as they had named the devilish network of Japanese strongpoints in their sector, and were even with the 3rd and the 5th. The surviving Japanese were pinned into the northernmost corner of the island, near Kitano Point.

We tried to persuade the Japanese to surrender. Japanese-American soldiers shouted down caves, and one of the few Japanese prisoners we had taken volunteered to carry a message through to one of the commanding officers. Nothing worked. Kuribayashi was determined to die with all his men.

In a gorge southeast of Kitano Point, the Japanese had built a gigantic concrete igloo. After two days of trying to take it, our infantrymen turned the job over to the engineers, who blew it up with 8500 pounds of explosives. How many Japanese soldiers died there —to no avail—was never known.

On the last day, March 26th, some of the Japanese —the few who were still alive—attempted one final counterattack. It lasted three hours. When it was finished, Iwo Jima was ours.

Exactly 6,821 Americans had died in the bloodiest battle in the history of the Marine Corps.

At the same time, Iwo had already begun to save lives. Thirty-six of our Superfortresses had already made emergency landings on the Iwo airfields. And before the end of the war, which was only five months off, the total number of such landings was to add up to 2,251.

That meant that almost 25,000 pilots and crew members, who might have been forced to crash-land in the vast stretches of the Pacific, put down safely on the battered little island.

One Air Force man, writing for a service magazine, told what it meant:

"Iwo broke the long stretch coming and going. If you had engine trouble, you held out for Iwo. If you were shot up over Japan and had wounded aboard, you held out for Iwo. If the weather was too rough, you held out for Iwo. Formations assembled over Iwo, and gassed up at Iwo for extra-long missions. If you needed fighter escort, it usually came from Iwo. If you had to ditch or bail out, you knew that air-sea rescue units were sent from Iwo. Even if you never used Iwo as an emergency base, it was a psychological benefit. It was there to fall back on."

A B-29 "Superfortress" comes in for a landing on an Iwo Jima airstrip.

9

Okinawa: The Next-to-Last Step

We had one more island to conquer before we and
our allies could invade Japan: Okinawa, in the Ryukyu
Islands, 350 miles south of Japan.

The Allied strategists had abandoned their plans to
take Formosa. The Japanese army in China had overrun the sites we had hoped to use as air bases, and we
had thought of taking Formosa as a prelude to landing
in China. Now that the war in Europe was approaching its end, the Allied leaders decided to proceed directly toward Japan. Okinawa was big enough to serve
as a troop staging area for the final invasion of Japan.
It could be developed into a great naval and air base,
and its capture would bring all the major industrial

cities of Japan within range of American medium bombers.

On the day Iwo Jima fell—March 26th—the 77th Infantry Division landed successfully on a cluster of small islands called the Kerama Retto some twenty-five miles west of Okinawa. Not more than a thousand Japanese had been left to defend them. General Mitsuru Ushijima, the Japanese commander, had stationed most of his men in the rugged terrain at the south end of Okinawa itself, for he was determined to make the Americans pay the heaviest possible price for their conquest. Concentration of his troops in the most favorable defensive position was the way to do that. So the 77th had a surprisingly easy time taking Kerama Retto.

In and around Kerama, however, we discovered some ominous Japanese equipment—350 suicide boats. They were an assortment of small wooden craft, heavily loaded with high explosives and designed for use against our invasion fleet. The Japanese had expected the suicide boats' skippers to ram our ships, blowing themselves up in attempts to sink our vessels.

These boats were a hint of the Japanese plans for Okinawa's defense.

The pattern of the main American assault landing on April 1st included everything we had learned about the difficult technique in more than three years

HEDO CAPE

IE SHIMA

AIR FIELD

MOTOBU PENIN.

NAGO BAY

O K I N A W A

CHIMU BAY

YONTAN FIELD

HAGUSHI

KADENA FIELD

HAGUSHI BAY

GINOWAN

MACHINATO

NAKAGUSUKU BAY

NAHA

SHURI

YONABARU

ARAGACHI

ITOMAN

CAPE CHAMU

PACIFIC OCEAN

of constant practice. This time we had more of everything than ever before. Lieutenant General Simon
B. Buckner's Tenth Army contained four divisions—
the 1st and 6th Marines and the 7th and 96th Infantry
—in addition to the 77th. Those four made the attack, while the 77th, after mopping up on the Kerama
Islands, got ready to take Ie Island off the northwest
coast of Okinawa.

For the first four days everything went smoothly.
We had picked beaches near Hagushi so that we could
start right out by capturing two good airfields, at
Yontan and Kadena. The Japanese offered little resistance to our doing so.

Then the two Marine divisions turned left, and
streaked north, along both coasts, through the hilly,
heavily populated countryside. In nine days—by April
13th—they had reached Hedo Cape at Okinawa's
northernmost tip.

A week later, Ie was in 77th Division hands—and
Ernie Pyle, America's best-known war correspondent,
was dead. He had accompanied the 77th to Ie, following the fighting men closely, as he had throughout
the war. A Japanese soldier with an automatic weapon
had slipped through the American lines and killed
him. Pyle lies buried in the American cemetery on Ie
beside the soldiers he wrote about.

The situation in the south was entirely different.

After the beachhead was established, the 96th and the 7th turned right. They promptly ran into the outpost line of Ushijima's concentrated defense-in-depth. The situation was like Iwo Jima—perhaps even worse. It wasn't hard to see that, once again, we were going to be forced to slog our way foot by foot.

As if that weren't bad enough, the Japanese now made painfully clear the fact that suicide was their one remaining strategy.

It was past time for their war leaders to surrender. Except for a brief pause to support the Okinawa landings, our air assault on Japan had steadily mounted in both intensity and precision. Not a shred of hope for Japan remained. But the Japanese government was in the hands of fanatics, and they had concocted an insane plan to kill a maximum number of men on both sides.

We had already seen a great many Japanese suicide attacks, especially during the battles for Leyte and Luzon. Japanese pilots, instead of releasing their bombs, had flown their bomb-laden planes directly into their targets. We hadn't quite realized, until the middle of March, the role that Japan had assigned these "Kamikaze" fliers. Then, when one of our carrier task forces had been attacking the Japanese mainland, swarms of Kamikaze planes had attacked it. Five of our carriers—the *Franklin,* the *Hancock,*

A Kamikaze attack caused this tremendous hole in the deck of the USS Bunker Hill.

the *Intrepid,* the *Wasp,* and the *Enterprise*—had been hit and damaged.

Japanese propaganda insisted that the pilots of Kamikaze planes had all volunteered to die. We know now that, like so much Japanese propaganda, this was a lie. Every week every air base in Japan was ordered to select a draft of Kamikaze pilots. The commanding officers began by taking the least skillful, or the oldest, or the youngest, of their men. No Kamikaze could refuse: he would have been shot. The Kamikaze planes were the worst the Japanese had left, many of them outmoded models or training planes.

When a flight of Kamikaze set out to attack, it was led by first-class non-Kamikaze planes, whose job was to make sure the suicide pilots did their "duty." The Kamikaze pilots had no chance to escape, because their own comrades—in faster ships—would have gunned them down.

At least one Kamikaze pilot protested, at the cost of his life. He crashed his airplane into the hangar of his own air base, which caught fire, destroying the planes remaining in it. A suicide note among his possessions explained that he had done it to save the lives of the pilots who would have been forced to fly the planes on suicidal missions.

After we had landed on Okinawa, the Japanese sent Kamikaze planes to destroy our invasion fleet and the warships supporting the operation. Our radar picket ships tried to warn the rest of our navy—and became the suicide bombers' first targets. We threw up a storm of anti-aircraft fire, and blanketed our ships with smoke screens, but invariably some of the Kamikazes got through. They were inaccurate, but there were hundreds of them. They hit our hospital ships as well as military targets, but no one ever knew whether the Kamikaze pilots could see what they were doing.

On April 6th, while a non-suicide attack occupied the attention of United States Task Force 58, two hundred Kamikaze attacked the transports off Hagushi in a strike that lasted for five terrible hours. One crash-bombed the picket-destroyer *Bush*. The destroyer *Calhoun*, coming to the aid of her sinking sister ship, was hit by four Kamikaze. The raid killed ninety-four Americans, sank six of our ships, and damaged another eighteen. Yet Japan's only real accomplishment in all this death and destruction—the only practical military gain—was sinking an ammunition ship that carried all the re-supply of 81-millimeter mortar ammunition for American forces ashore.

The Japanese had also planned a suicide attack for the pride of the Japanese navy, the battleship *Yamato*, which had escaped from the battles around Leyte. The *Yamato*, with an escort of one light cruiser and eight destroyers, was given enough fuel for a one-way trip to Okinawa. When she arrived, she was supposed to turn her batteries of heavy guns on the American ships, while Kamikaze planes attacked overhead, and to sink as many as she could before, as was inevitable, she was sunk herself.

The *Yamato* steamed out of the inland waters between the Japanese islands and headed for the open sea. Two American submarines, the *Hackleback* and the *Threadfin,* were lying submerged right off the Japanese coast. They spotted the *Yamato,* and alerted the Fifth Fleet.

Task Force 58 launched 386 planes. Their mission: sink the *Yamato.* On the first attempt our planes hit the great battleship with two bombs and a torpedo, but she stayed afloat. One of her escort destroyers went down, and the cruiser was stopped dead in the water. Our next strike did the job. Three more bombs and nine more torpedoes struck the *Yamato.* She turned over in the water and exploded, a full day's sail away from her target off Okinawa.

Ushijima's ground defense was suicide in a more orthodox form. He had taught his soldiers that each Japanese was to trade his life for the lives of ten Americans, or for one American tank. The southern end of Okinawa was like a deadly ant hill, full of secret tunnels connecting gun positions and holding stores of ammunition. The Japanese had all the short-range weapons—mortars, machine guns, and a light artillery —they could use. In a land of draws, ravines, gullies, ridges and hills they had little need of long-range guns.

Day after day, we crawled forward. Ushijima had three strong defensive lines in the mountainous ground around Shuri, and, as slowly as possible, he fell back from one to the next. The United States 96th Division was chewed to ribbons, and the 27th, which had been in reserve, came into the line. The 77th and the 1st Marines came down from the north to join the battle.

On the fourth of May—a month from the day the attack had begun—Ushijima made a mistake. He let his subordinate officer talk him into a major counter-attack. It failed and it cost the Japanese 6,000 casualties.

By the end of May, at a frightful cost, we finally took the city of Shuri; and Ushijima retreated farther south to the high ground around Kiyamu, where he had stock-piled weapons for his last-ditch fight. He had only eight square miles of Okinawa left to defend.

Buckner radioed Ushijima and asked him to surrender. Ushijima refused.

Our attack began at three in the morning of June 12th, and the battle was furious. By the night of June 17th, we had captured all the important terrain features around Ushijima's last stronghold. On the 18th we started our final assault. General Buckner visited an American observation post, drew Japanese artillery fire, and was killed. But he had lived long enough to know that he had won the battle for Okinawa.

The next day, in the cave which served as his head-

A wounded soldier is helped back to the rear for medical attention.

quarters, Ushijima dictated his farewell orders. He told his men to try to disguise themselves as Okinawans —perhaps they would have a chance, later, to harass the Americans. But the Japanese had been told so many lies, and witnessed so much useless death, that many of them, in spite of their orders, surrendered.

At three o'clock in the morning of June 22nd, Ushijima stepped out of his cave onto a little ledge overhanging the ocean. An advancing American patrol was less than 100 feet away on top of a hill. In the presence of a few remaining members of his staff, Ushijima committed hara-kiri.

His suicide coincided with one last big Kamikaze attack. Suicide pilots attacked all night, hitting a number of our ships. But at dawn the General was dead, the Kamikaze were dead, and the Americans held Okinawa.

The only thing to be said for Ushijima was that he had done what he intended: he had turned the defense of Okinawa into one of the costliest battles in all history. He had lost 117,000 men—110,000 of them dead. He had spent 7,830 airplanes, the Kamikaze planes included.

American losses, while not nearly so high, were terrible to contemplate; more than 49,000 casualties, including 12,520 killed in action.

10

Japan Surrenders

We immediately set about the great job of turning Okinawa into an all-purpose base for the invasion of Japan, although we hoped that the enemy would abandon its policy of national suicide. Japan's surrender was past due.

In March, Major General Curtis LeMay—who, after the capture of Iwo Jima, could provide his Superfortresses with fighter-plane protection—had adopted a new policy. He began to send our planes to bomb Japan at the low level of 7,000 feet, instead of much higher, and at night, instead of in the daytime. In place of high explosives, we dropped incendiary bombs designed to start fires. Our aim was to demolish Japan's cities, starting with the biggest.

For more than two months we bombed Tokyo, Nagoya, Osaka, Kobe, and Yokohama. By the middle of June, 100 square miles of densely populated ground —the heart of these six cities—had been burned out. In Tokyo alone, 3,000,000 persons were homeless.

There was still no sign that the Japanese war leaders had had enough—or that the Japanese people could overthrow the madmen in control of their destiny— so we turned our attention to the next sixty most important Japanese cities.

Day after day, fewer and fewer Japanese planes rose to intercept our vast air armadas. The Japanese had squandered pilots and planes on Kamikaze raids. Now the Japanese aircraft industry was rapidly being destroyed by our air power.

The war in Europe had ended on May 8th, at 11:01 P.M., a week after Hitler had committed suicide at his ruined chancellery in Berlin. That same day—VE (Victory in Europe) Day—the Allies called on Japan to surrender, too. Admiral Baron Kantaro Suzuki, by then, had formed Japan's third wartime government, replacing Koiso. Suzuki was supposed to be a moderate. At least, he had not been a member of Japan's powerful, war-minded army clique. But his government ignored the Allied ultimatum.

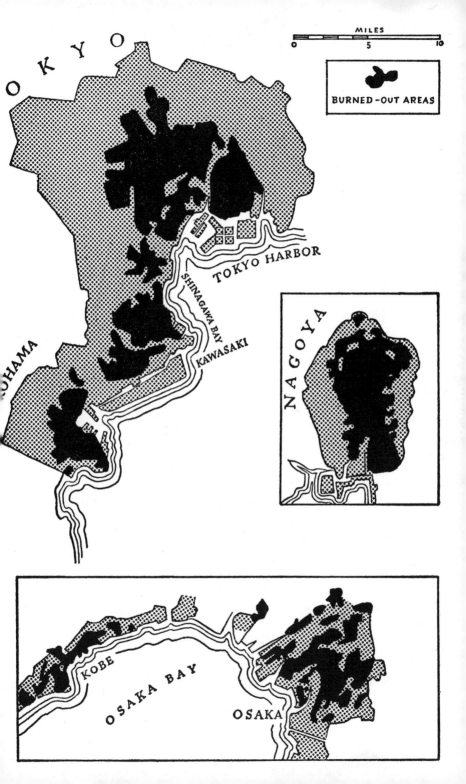

Late in July, the heads of the nations who had been victorious in Europe—President Harry S. Truman (who had taken office in April, when Franklin Roosevelt died), Prime Minister Winston Churchill, and Premier Josef Stalin—met to confer at Potsdam, Germany.

They agreed that Japan should "be given an opportunity" to end the war and promised that the Allies would not humiliate Emperor Hirohito. The Potsdam Declaration, published on July 26th, was broadcast repeatedly so that the Japanese people could hear it, and it was formally delivered through neutral "diplomatic channels," the representatives of Switzerland and Sweden in Tokyo.

Japan's reaction was to denounce the Allied offer as "absurd," "presumptuous," and "unworthy of consideration."

That left us no choice. Our bombings continued, while the Allies moved great quantities of military equipment, and millions of soldiers, sailors, and airmen, from the European to the Pacific theater. Many of our warships had arrived even before Germany's defeat. Now the British navy was free to join them. A whole British battle fleet fell in with Halsey's Third Fleet, ranging along the Japanese coasts, shelling and bombing every military target it could find. (For some Australian soldiers, the switch meant a return to their home hemisphere. Despite her long years of danger, Australia had sent many of her best troops to Europe.)

Allied commanders and their staffs worked out detailed plans for the Japanese invasion. We intended to land on Kyushu in November; then, if all went well, our second assault, on Honshu, at a point just south of Tokyo, would take place in March, 1946. We estimated that the Japanese had 2,500,000 soldiers in the home islands, although it was impossible to say just what effect our air-and-naval pounding had had upon their morale and their equipment. In Okinawa the Japanese had rounded up Okinawan high-school boys to fight our invasion. We feared that, to defend Japan proper, the government might call on old men and boys and women of all ages to fight like soldiers.

The Allied planners expected that our forces would suffer one million casualties in the invasion of Japan.

But the men who worked out these plans did not know that the United States and Great Britain had just developed a fantastic secret weapon: the atom bomb.

Our scientists had been working on it in the greatest secrecy throughout the war. Ironically, many of the Allied physicists and mathematicians who had done the job were German and Italian refugees, driven from their homes by Hitler and Mussolini. They and

A Japanese city in flames after an American air attack.

their English and American colleagues had known for some time that the atom could be split. They had feared that Germany might solve the problems in the way of making a practical atomic bomb, and so control more explosive power than had ever been dreamed of. Albert Einstein, then the most famous scientist in the world, on behalf of a number of his colleagues, wrote President Roosevelt, to warn him of that possibility.

Our government—and Great Britain's, too—was slow to understand what the scientists' warning meant.

To non-scientists the idea was incredible. And soldiers and statesmen were not yet sure we could build enough conventional weapons, planes, ships, and tanks to win the war. Spending time and money on an atom bomb that might not work seemed terribly risky. For a time English and American scientists continued to experiment on their own. Then the United States invested a small sum to test whether an atomic "chain reaction" was really possible—whether one atom, splitting, could trigger another to split, and so on, making a huge explosion. Enrico Fermi, an Italian refugee, directed our team of scientific investigators. In December, 1942—a year after Pearl Harbor—his experiment had succeeded.

It still wasn't certain that a practical bomb could be built. We might waste a fortune—and, more important, our best scientific brains—on a failure. We took the chance.

The British agreed that the work had to be done in the United States because England was being constantly bombed by Germany. General Leslie Groves, an Army engineer, was put in charge of the top-secret "Manhattan Project," a phrase that meant nothing. Three hidden cities were built, in Tennessee, Washington, and New Mexico, to house the work. Almost no one knew what it was all about. Famous scientists vanished from our universities. They moved, with their families, into these queer towns that had appeared out of nowhere. The work was divided up so that most of the men hadn't the faintest idea what they were doing, except the specific task assigned them. In all, the bomb cost more than $2,000,000,000, and Undersecretary of War Robert P. Patterson, who paid out this enormous sum, didn't know what it was being spent for.

On July 16th, ten days before the Potsdam Declaration, the first atomic bomb was exploded on the desert near Los Alamos, New Mexico. It worked so well, and its explosive power was so great—equal to 20,000 tons of T.N.T.—that our scientist-observers were terrified in the midst of their rejoicing.

Churchill, in Germany, agreed with Truman that if the Japanese refused to surrender after hearing our lenient Potsdam offer, we ought to drop the atomic bomb. But there was no escaping the fact that our President, by himself, had to give the orders that sent our Superfortress, the *Enola Gay,* on its way from the airstrip on Tinian Island to the target city, Hiroshima.

At nine o'clock in the morning, August 6, 1945, when the big plane appeared, the residents of Hiroshima paid little attention. They had been used to seeing such great formations of American bombers in the sky that one B-29 scarcely seemed dangerous.

At exactly 9:15, the bomb, with a parachute attached, dropped from the plane and floated down. The explosion began with a pinpoint of light that grew, faster than anyone could see, into a gigantic fireball half a mile across. The thunderous blast was heard hundreds of miles away. Great rings of smoke rose into a column 10,000 feet high, which gradually assumed the shape of a huge mushroom five times taller than that. At the mushroom's base, hidden for the moment in steaming clouds, sixty percent of the city had been obliterated.

About 100,000 were dead or fatally injured—an exact count was impossible because some of those exposed to the bomb's radioactive effect did not die for a long time afterwards.

Immediately after bombing Hiroshima we dropped

millions of leaflets explaining exactly what had happened, and begging the Japanese to force their government to surrender.

On August 8th, Russia declared war against Japan, and Russian troops moved into Japanese-held Manchuria.

On August 9th, the Third Fleet made another great raid on Honshu, and a second atom bomb was dropped, this time on Nagasaki.

Once again, on August 10th, Truman called on the Japanese to give up. This time, under great pressure from the Emperor, the government did so.

The Pacific Fleet moved into Tokyo Bay, still not sure that the Emperor's decision would be obeyed by Japan's armed forces. But it was.

General MacArthur, who had been named commander of the Japanese invasion, accepted Japan's formal surrender on board Halsey's flagship, the *Missouri,* on September 2nd.

Japan's dreams of military conquest had ended. Her oppression of the countries of Asia was finished, and so was the misrule of the Japanese people by their own militarists.

One small ceremony remained. A week later, MacArthur, with General Eichelberger, visited the American Embassy in Tokyo. The generals watched an American flag raised on the Embassy flagpole. It had

A Japanese watches U.S. troops making an unopposed landing at Waka-yama, Japan, shortly after his country's surrender.

a special significance. It was the very flag that had been flying at the Capitol in Washington, D.C., on December 7, 1941.

"Let it wave in its full glory," MacArthur said, "as a symbol of hope for the oppressed and as a harbinger of victory for the right."

The official Japanese surrender aboard the USS Missouri, September 2, 1945. Shown at the left is General of the Army Douglas MacArthur.

Index

From Pearl Harbor to Okinawa